D0844881

THE HORSE'S NAME WAS . . .

A dictionary of
famous horses from history, literature,
mythology, television and movies

by
Terri A. Wear

The Scarecrow Press, Inc.
Metuchen, N.J., & London
1993

British Library Cataloguing-in-Publication data available

Library of Congress Cataloging-in-Publication Data

Wear, Terri A., 1951–
    The horse's name was . . . : a dictionary of famous horses
from history, literature, mythology, television and movies / by
Terri A. Wear.
        p.   cm.
    Includes bibliographical references (p.) and index.
    ISBN 0–8108–2599–6 (acid-free paper)
    1. Horses—Dictionaries.   2. Horses—Names—Dictionaries.
I. Title.
SF278.W43   1993
636.1—dc20   92–37724

Manufactured in the United States of America

Printed on acid-free paper

CONTENTS

PREFACE

There have been horses in all aspects of life since the horse became domesticated. Horses are found in mythology, ridden in war, kept as pets, star in movies and television, are part of civilization, and have had a spot in the hearts of people for a long time. Some of these horses became famous: some due to a part they played in history, some due to who their owners were, and some because a movie or television program became popular. Many of these horses are known to everyone, like Black Beauty, Trigger, Man O'War, and Pegasus. And there are many whose names have been forgotten or were never known. Paul Revere's mount, which carried him and his message during Revolutionary times, is one of those. History tells us that his mount for that famous ride was most likely a mare, but her name is generally considered to be unknown.

This book was written to preserve the memory of some of these famous horses and their names. The horses listed here are those that have for some reason been recognized for their achievements, their race records, their bravery in battle, their screen performances, their part in literature, and even for their heroic acts.

Horses' names are listed alphabetically in capital letters with their reasons for fame following. Owners' names, people associated with the horses, movie and book titles, etc., are integrated alphabetically in regular type and refer the reader to the appropriate horse(s). If more than one horse is listed with the same name, the cross-reference will also include the entry number for the appropriate citation. A bibliography of books for further reading follows the Dictionary, along with a subject index.

As with any list of names, this one cannot be and does not claim to be comprehensive. Any breed fancier, sport enthusiast, history buff, or literature expert will undoubtedly feel that some famous horses are missing. That is probably true. I apologize to those persons and to the memory of those horses. I hope that the book will fill a need for many readers. It should be of interest to horse lovers of all kinds, to crossword puzzle enthusiasts, trivia collectors, historians, movie buffs, and to librarians.

THE DICTIONARY

1. AARON—A black horse belonging to writer D.H. Lawrence. When AARON died, Lawrence had his hide made into a duffel bag.

   Abartha (The Hard Servant)—see THE MEAN MARE.

2. ABASTER—One of the four black horses belonging to Pluto in classical mythology. Name means "deprived of the light of day."

3. ABATOS—One of the four black horses belonging to Pluto in classical mythology. Name means "inaccessible."

   Abbott and Costello—see TEABISCUIT.

4. ABD EL KADER—A small horse, 15.2 hands, that won the Grand National Steeplechase in 1850 and 1851. He was the first horse to win it twice and in successive years.

5. ABDALLAH—The sire of HAMBLETONIAN, he had a reputation as a killer.

6. ABDUL—A Greek burro used to carry wounded soldiers during World War I.

7. ABE EDGINGTON—One of four horses photographed by Eadweard Muybridge in the 1870s to show that all four feet of a horse come off the ground when galloping.

   Abernathy, Louis and Templeton—see GERONIMO, SAM (1028).

1

8. ABOVE SUSPICION—A racehorse belonging to Queen Elizabeth II that she withdrew from a race in 1959. The queen was fined for doing so.

9. ACE—One of cowboy movie star, Tim McCoy's horses.

10. ACE—A black horse that Tom Tyler rode early in his western movie career.

Achilles—see BALIUS, XANTHUS (1296).

Acord, Art—see BLACK BEAUTY (132).

11. ADIOS—A Standardbred stallion, foaled in 1940, that influenced the breed.

ADMIRAL—see WAR ADMIRAL.

Adrastus—see ARION, CERUS.

"The Adventures of Champion," television show—see CHAMPION, LINDY, TONY JR.

The Adventures of Rex and Rinty, movie—see REX (973).

"The Adventures of Silver Blaze," short story—see SILVER BLAZE.

12. AETHON—One of the wild white horses belonging to Apollo/Helios, the sun god in classical mythology, that pulled his chariot across the sky. Name means "heavenly fire." Apollo's half-human son, Phaeton, once tried to drive the sun horses across the sky and failed.

13. AETHON—One of Hector's chariot horses in Homer's *Iliad.*

14. AETHON—One of Athena's horses in classical mythology.

15. AETON—One of the four black horses belonging to Pluto in classical mythology. Name means "swift as an eagle."

16. AFFIRMED—The 1978 Triple Crown winner, a chestnut colt.

Agba—see SHAM.

17. AGILE—The 1905 Kentucky Derby winner, a brown colt, in a Derby field of three horses.

Aguecheek, Sir Andrew—see CAPILET.

AH-CHIM-HAI—see RECKLESS.

18. AHLERICH—A Westphalian warmblood, foaled in 1971, that became the World Champion dressage horse under well-known German dressage rider Reiner Klimke in 1982. Klimke purchased the big bay with a white blaze and two white socks in 1975. The horse was 13 when they won the Individual Dressage at the 1984 Olympics in Los Angeles.

Ainsworth, William Harrison, author—see BLACK BESS (135).

19. AJAX—A horse ridden by Confederate General Robert E. Lee early in the Civil War. AJAX was too big for Lee and was sent back to the farm, where he was killed in an accident when he ran into the iron prong of a gate latch.

Alamo, Battle of—see UNKNOWN HORSE (1232).

20. ALAN-A-DALE—The 1902 Kentucky Derby winner, a chestnut colt. His jockey was Jimmy Winkfield, the last black person to ride a winner in the Kentucky Derby.

21. ALASTOR—One of Pluto's horses in classical mythology.

22. ALBATROSS—A well-known pacer in the 1970s.

Albert Edward, Prince of Wales—see PERSIMMON.

23. AL BORAK—The mythical winged white mare that carried Muhammad from earth to the seventh heaven in Muslim legend. Muhammad, or Mahomet, was the founder of Islam in the 7th century. The horse was said to have a human head and possess dazzling splendor and incredible speed. Also spelled EL BARAT, or EL BORAK, or BORAK. Name means "lightning."

24. ALCADE—A Thoroughbred stallion, first in team tying in 1946.

25. ALCOCK ARABIAN—All gray Thoroughbreds are descended from this horse, which lived around 1720.

26. ALDANITI—The winner of the 1981 Grand National steeplechase with Bob Champion as his jockey. Before the race, Champion had made a comeback from cancer and Aldaniti from a serious leg injury.

27. ALDEBARAN—One of the four Arabian stallions driven by Charlton Heston in the 1959 movie *Ben-Hur,* based on the book by Lew Wallace. All four were named after stars. The were owned, in the story, by the Sheik Ilderim and were bright bays in the book and white in the movie.

28. ALEXANDER—Queen Elizabeth II's racehorse that won the 1955 2,000 Guineas Trial Stakes and was the first of three consecutive winners of that race for her.

Alexander the Great—see BUCEPHALUS.

29. ALFANA—The clever mare belonging to Gradasso in the Charlemagne legend. Name means "mare."

30. ALGONQUIN—A calico Icelandic pony owned by Archibald Roosevelt while his father, Theodore, was president of the United States. Once when Archibald was sick, the pony was taken upstairs in the White House to his bedroom by his brother.

31. ALI—One of Napoleon Bonaparte's favorite white warhorses.

    Ali—see DHULDUL.

32. ALICE-OF-THE-NIGHT—A horse belonging to King Richard I, (the Lion-Hearted), a black mare that carried Richard's body from the battlefield.

    ALIGERO CLAVILENO—see CLAVILENO.

    Al Khamseh—see DAHMA, HADBA, HAMDANIEH, SAQLAWIEH, UBAYYAH.

33. ALLAHMANDE—One of George Patton's horses, a chestnut gelding show horse, foaled in 1917.

    ALLAN F-1—see BLACK ALLAN.

    Allen, Rex—see KOKO.

34. ALLERTON—A leading Thoroughbred sire in the early 1900s.

    All's Well That Ends Well, play—see CURTAL.

35. ALSAB—An unfashionably bred racehorse that was purchased for $700. He is said to have been overworked and badly managed, but he won many races and earned $350,015 in his career. He match-raced WHIRLAWAY in the 1940s, and while it looked like both crossed the finish line at the same time, ALSAB was awarded the win.

36. ALSVID—Pulled the sun across the sky with ARVAK in Norse mythology.

37. ALSVIDER—A milk-white mare that pulled the moon across the sky for Mani the moon goddess in Norse legend. Also spelled ALSVIDUR.

ALYDAR—see ALYSHEBA.

38. ALYFAR—One of Arthur Godfrey's Arabian stallions.

39. ALYSHEBA—The 1987 Kentucky Derby winner, a bay colt, sired by ALYDAR. ALYSHEBA was jostled by another horse and stumbled almost to his knees. He recovered without falling and went on to win the race.

AMERICAN ECLIPSE—see ECLIPSE (AMERICAN).

American Expeditionary Force—see PUTNAM.

40. AMETHEA—One of the horses belonging to Helios, the sun god, in classical mythology.

41. AMIGO—The genuine palomino pony owned by radio star Bobby Benson.

"And Her Name Was Maud," comic strip—see MAUD (749).

42. ANDALOUSE—General Jean Baptiste Jules Bernadotte's sorrel war-horse in the 1813 Battle of Leipzig. Bernadotte later ruled Sweden and Norway as King Charles XIV John.

Anderson, C.W., author—see BLAZE.

43. ANDREW JACKSON—A fast early day trotter.

Andrew, Prince—see MR. DINKUM, VALKYRIE.

44. ANDY—One of the Budweiser Clydesdale geldings from the eight-horse hitch that toured the western states.

45. ANGELINA—A 2-year-old Dartmoor pony filly, one of five horses that Velvet inherited from Mr. Cellini in Enid Bagnold's book, *National Velvet*.

Animal Farm, book—see BENJAMIN, BOXER, CLO-VER, MOLLIE.

46. ANNA—Rudolph Valentino's horse's real name in the 1921 movie, *The Sheik*.

Anna Karenina, book—see FROU FROU.

Anne, Princess—see ARTHUR OF TROY, BANDIT, COLUMBUS, DOUBLET, GOODWILL, HIGH JINKS, PRIDE, PURPLE STAR.

"Annie Oakley," television show—see BUTTERCUP, TARGET.

Ansara, Michael—see SHEIK.

47. ANTARES—One of the four Arabian stallions driven by Charlton Heston in the 1959 movie *Ben-Hur*, based on the book by Lew Wallace. All four were named after stars. They were owned by Sheik Ilderim and were bright bays in the book and white in the movie.

48. AONBHARR—A magical horse in Irish mythology that could travel both on land and on sea.

49. APACHE—One of the horses Kit Carson rode while he was Fremont's messenger from California to Washington, D.C., in the 1840s.

50. APACHE—Cowboy Bob Baker's black-and-white pinto horse in western movies.

51. APOLLO—The 1882 Kentucky Derby winner, a chestnut gelding.

Apollo—see AETHON (12), EOUS, PHLEGON, PYROIS.

52. APUKWA—A prizewinning Clydesdale horse.

53. ARAB—The gray Arabian polo pony ridden by Winston Churchill when he was with the Lancers in Egypt fighting Khalifa's army.

54. ARABELLE—Actress Hayley Mills' pony when she was young.

Arabian Nights—see THE EBONY HORSE.

Arane, Nikki—see RED LIGHTNING.

Arcaro, Eddie—see CITATION, HILL GAIL, HOOP JR., LAWRIN, WHIRLAWAY.

55. ARDIOS BUTLER—Won the harness racing Triple Crown in 1959 and was the first pacer to do so. He was retired to stud in 1961.

Ares—see DEIMOS, PHOBOS.

56. ARION—The fabulous winged stallion with a black mane that was the offspring of Demeter and Poseidon/Neptune in classical mythology. He was owned by Adrastus, later was given to Hercules, and was the first horse given to man. He was a talking horse and with CERUS pulled a chariot for Adrastus. Their story is told in Homer's *Iliad*.

57. ARISTIDES—Winner of the first Kentucky Derby, in 1875. He was a chestnut colt ridden by black jockey Oliver Lewis.

Arizona, movie—see DICE.

Arizona Bound, movie—see FLASH (438).

58. ARIZONA PIE—The last offspring of THE PIE, which belonged to Velvet Brown's niece Sarah in the movie *International Velvet,* based on the book by Bryan Forbes, sequel to *National Velvet* by Enid Bagnold.

59. ARKLE—A great Irish steeplechaser foaled in 1957, a bay gelding, that won three consecutive Cheltenham Gold Cups between 1964 and 1966. He was put down in 1970 due to a broken bone.

60. ARMED—A great racehorse, a brown gelding.

61. ARTERXERXES—XERXES and ARTERXERXES were two horses belonging to the large, enthusiastic foxhunter John Jorrocks in the popular novels by Robert S. Surtees in the 1840s and 1850s. ARTERXERXES was a very slow and clumsy jumper, but very patient with Jorrocks. He was so named because when the horses were driven in tandem, ARTERXERXES came behind XERXES or "arter" him.

Arthur, King—see CABALL, LAMRI, SPUMADOR.

62. ARTHUR OF TROY—One of Princess Anne's eventing horses.

63. ARUNDEL—English knight, Sir Bevis of Southampton's incomparable steed whose deeds are recorded in many poems. The name means "swallow" and he was as swift as a swallow.

64. ARVAK—With ALSVID, pulls the sun across the sky in Norse mythology. Name means "early walker."

65. ASHBY—One of Confederate Henry Douglas's horses in the Civil War, a black horse.

66. ASPERCEL—The show horse star of the 1968 Disney movie, *The Horse in the Gray Flannel Suit,* based on Eric Hatch's book, *Year of the Horse.*

The Asphalt Jungle, movie—see CORNCRACKER.

67. ASSAULT—The winner of the 1946 Triple Crown, a chestnut colt also known as THE CLUB-FOOTED COMET because of a deformed hoof, the result of a pasture accident as a colt in Texas. ASSAULT could not walk or trot very well, but he was sound and fast at the gallop. He was sterile, so he continued racing after the Triple Crown victory. He retired from racing in 1950 and died in Texas in 1971 at age 28.

Astley, Philip—see BILLY (123), GIBRALTAR.

At the Back of the North Wind, book—see DIAMOND.

68. ATAIR—One of the four Arabian stallions driven by Charlton Heston in the 1959 movie, *Ben-Hur*, based on the book by Lew Wallace. All four were named after stars, although ATAIR may represent the star Altair. Name means "flying eagle." The horses were owned by the Sheik Ilderim and were bright bays in the book and white horses in the movie.

Athena—see AETHON (14).

Auel, Jean, author—see RACER, WHINNEY.

69. AUREOLE—One of Queen Elizabeth I's horses.

70. AUSTERLITZ—One of Napoleon Bonaparte's favorite white war-horses.

Autry, Gene—see CHAMPION, LINDY, PAL (871), TONY JR.

Ayla—see WHINNEY.

Aymon—see BAYARD.

71. AZRA—The 1892 Kentucky Derby winner, a bay colt.

72. BABA—A small Mexican burro Grace Kelly received as a gift from Clark Gable in 1953.

73. BABA LOOEY—The Mexican burro in the 1959 TV cartoon show, "The Quick Draw McGraw Show."

74. BABIECA—The white war-horse belonging to the Spanish warrior-knight Rodrigo in the 11th century. Rodrigo was nicknamed el Sidi or El Cid Campeador. BABIECA, also spelled BAVIECA, means "idiot" or "dumbbell," and El Cid named him that when people called him an idiot for choosing the scraggly colt. BABIECA was made to carry his dead master's body, strapped upright in the saddle, from a besieged city, which made the enemy think that El Cid had risen from the dead. BABIECA lived to be 40 years old and died 2 ½ years after his master.

75. BABY—One of the horses that pulled the Overland Stage in the 1939 movie, *Stagecoach,* starring John Wayne. Andy Devine drove the stagecoach and shouted encouragement to the horses. There were three hitches of six horses each used on the stagecoach route.

Bacharach, Burt—see HEARTLIGHT NO. ONE.

76. BADEN-BADEN—Winner of the 1877 Kentucky Derby, a chestnut colt.

Bagnold, Enid, author—see ANGELINA, FANCY, GEORGE, MISS ADA, MRS. JAMES, THE PIE (907), SIR PERICLES.

Baker, Bob—see APACHE (50).

77. BALA—A horse in *King Solomon's Horses* by Nora Benjamin Kubie.

78. BALAAM'S ASS—An ass given the power of speech by the Lord after being struck three times by its rider, in the Bible, Numbers 22:21–35.

Balch, Glenn, author—see INKY, KING (632).

79. BALDY—The best calf-roping horse from 1936 to 1949 foaled in Tulsa, Oklahoma. His first owner was Clyde Burk. BALDY was badly burned in a trailer fire in his first year on the rodeo circuit, but recovered and went on to win championships with three different owners. The 15.1-hand, 1,080-pound scar-legged sorrel died in 1961 of natural causes. He is buried under a monument at the Jake McClure Rodeo Arena in Lovington, New Mexico.

80. BALDY—One of Union General George Meade's war-horses during the Civil War, a Saddle Horse type that could rack. He was a bright bay with a white blaze and white socks. He was shot several times but always recovered. He was led in Meade's funeral procession in 1872, and when he died in 1882 his head and forefeet were mounted as relics.

81. BALIUS—The horse born of Zephyrus and the Harpy Podarge in classical mythology. The name means "dappled" and is also spelled BALIOS. Along with XAN-THUS, he drew Achilles' chariot and was immortal. Their story is told in Homer's *Iliad*.

Baltimore Colts—see NEWCOMER.

82. BANDIT—A Welsh pony owned by Prince Charles that was also ridden by his sister, Princess Anne, when they were children.

The "Bandit Queen"—see VENUS.

Bandolero, movie—see PIE (906).

83. BANJO—Lucky Jenkins' horse in Hopalong Cassidy movies.

Banks, General Nathaniel—see CHARLIE (256), SHEN-ANDOAH.

Banks, Thomas—see MAROCCO.

84. BANNER—Flicka's wild sire in Mary O'Hara's books *My Friend Flicka* and *Thunderhead*.

85. BANNER—Bob Steele's favorite sorrel horse, which he rode in early western movies.

86. BARAKAT—An Arabian ridden by Tyrone Power in the 1938 movie *Suez*.

87. BARBAMOUCHE—Climborin's swift horse in the epic poem, *The Song of Roland*.

Barkley, Nick—see COCO (271).

Barkley, Victoria—see MISTY GIRL.

"Barney Google," comic strip—see SPARK PLUG.

Barney, Natalie Clifford—see TRICKSY.

88. BARNEY OWENS—A legendary sire of the American Quarter Horse, foaled around 1870.

89. BARNUM—A plow horse used by author Laura Ingalls Wilder after her marriage to Manly Wilder.

90. BARON—One of cowboy movie star Tim McCoy's horses.

91. BARON—Tom Tyler's white horse, which he rode late in his western movie career.

92. BARON REALIZATION—The well-known Budweiser Clydesdale stallion that was the star of television commercials and posters. Also called BARON.

Barrett, Lawrence, author—see TWINKLE.

Bass, Tom—see BELLE BEACH, MISS REX, MR. POTTS.

93. BATAILLE—The old white pit pony that dies in Emile Zola's *Germinal.*

Battell, Colonel Joseph—see JUSTIN MORGAN.

94. BATTLEFIELD—A well-known inbred racehorse.

95. BATTLESHIP—Man O'War's son, he won the Grand National steeplechase in 1938. He was the first American-bred and American-owned horse to win the Grand National. He was a small horse, 15.2 hands, and a stallion, one of the few stallions to win this race. His jockey was only 17 years old.

BAVIECA—see BABIECA.

96. BAYARD—A legendary bright bay demon horse of incredible speed owned by the four sons of Aymon in medieval romance. Rinaldo was one of the four brothers. BAYARD increased in size if two or more persons mounted him. Name means "bright bay."

97. BAYARD—Union General Philip Kearny's black horse, which he rode during the Civil War. Kearny was killed while mounted on BAYARD at the Battle of Chantilly.

Bayer, Carol—see HEARTLIGHT NO. ONE.

Beasts and Super-Beasts—see THE BROGUE.

98. BEAU—John Wayne's horse in the movies *True Grit,* 1969 (based on the novel by Charles Portis), and *Rooster Cogburn,* 1975. BEAU was played by a horse named DOLLAR.

99. BEAUREGARD—One of Confederate General Wade Hampton's war-horses in the Civil War. The 16.2-hand,

bold-spirited horse was presented to Hampton by General Beauregard and died in battle in 1863.

BEAUTIFUL BAY—see TRUE BRITON.

100. BEAUTY—A mare owned by actress Hayley Mills when she was a young girl.

101. BEAUTY—Adam Cartwright's horse in the television show "Bonanza," 1959–1973.

102. BEAUTY—The horse ridden by Joan Crawford in *Johnny Guitar*, 1954; Clark Gable in *Lone Star*, 1952; and Elizabeth Taylor in *Giant*, 1956.

Beauty and the Beast, film—see MAGNIFIQUE.

Beebe, Paul and Maureen—see MISTY (784), SEA STAR, STORMY (1134).

103. BEHAVE YOURSELF—The 1921 Kentucky Derby winner, a bay colt.

BEIFFROR—see BROIEFORT.

BELAIR BULLET—see OMAHA.

104. BELLBOY—Half-brother to COLUMBUS, both ridden by Queen Elizabeth II in the 1970s.

105. BELLE BEACH—One of the greatest high-school show mares in America, owned and trained by Tom Bass, a black horseman in the early 1900s.

106. BELLE OF ALL—A great polo pony at Meadowbrook, Long Island.

Bellerophon—see PEGASUS (886).

107. BELLFOUNDER—A Hackney horse, foaled in 1815, imported from England in 1822, and an influence on the American Hackney breed.

108. BELLINO II—A French trotter that had won $1,960,945 in the 1970s. He disliked flying in airplanes and could walk on his hind legs.

Belloc, Hilaire, author—see JACK (579), TOM THE POLO PONY.

109. BEN ALI—The 1886 Kentucky Derby winner, a brown colt.

110. BEN BRUSH—The 1896 Kentucky Derby winner, a bay colt, ridden by black jockey Willie Simms.

Ben-Hur, book and movie—see ALDEBARAN, ANTARES, ATAIR, EROS, MARS, RIGEL.

Ben: Story of a Cart Horse, see CAESAR (221).

111. BENIK—One of the four horses of the sun in Persian mythology. The other three were Enik, Menik, and Senik.

112. BENJAMIN—The bad-tempered old donkey in George Orwell's book *Animal Farm* that talked very little but always commented that "donkeys live a long time."

Bennett, Reese—see CACTUS.

Benson, Bobby—see AMIGO.

113. BEPPO—Charger belonging to Union General Judson Kilpatrick, who often hugged the sorrel horse. BEPPO was killed in the fighting at Aldie.

Bernadotte, Jean Baptiste Jules—see ANDALOUSE.

Berry, Erick, author—see UNKNOWN HORSE (1239)

114. BERTO—A blind stallion, one of several horses owned and trained by Karl Krall in Elberfeld, Germany, in the late 1800s and early 1900s, which could do mathematics. Scientists could find no fraud in the exhibition. See also KLUGE HANS.

115. BESSIE—One of the horses that pulled the Overland Stage in the 1939 movie, *Stagecoach,* starring John Wayne. Andy Devine drove the stage and shouted encouragement to the horses. There were three hitches of six horses each used on the stagecoach route.

116. BETSY—One of Queen Elizabeth II's favorite mounts, a black mare of little breeding. The queen rode the mare until the horse was in her 20s.

117. BETSY—The mare that Sam Hart raced against the devil and his black mare SALOME. Hart was given SALOME when he beat the devil, and then he neglected BETSY, according to an old New England folktale.

118. BETSY HARRISON—A dark bay mare, foaled in 1828, that greatly influenced the American Saddle Horse breed.

119. BEVIS—Lord Marmion's red roan steed, ridden in the battle at Flodden Field in Sir Walter Scott's poem *Marmion.* Name means "swift."

Bevis of Southampton, Sir—see ARUNDEL.

The Big Country, movie—see DOMINO (362), LITTLE JOHN.

BIG CY—see CITATION.

120. BIG JIM—A Clydesdale gelding standing 21.1 hands that was claimed to be the tallest horse. He was foaled in Scotland in 1950 and died in 1957.

BIG RED—see MAN O'WAR.

"The Big Valley," television show—see COCO (271), MISTY GIRL.

Biggs, John, Jr., author—see CORKRAN OF CLAM-STRETCH.

121. BILL—One of the Budweiser Clydesdale geldings from the eight-horse hitch that toured the fourteen western states.

122. BILL—One of the horses that pulled the Overland Stage in the 1939 movie *Stagecoach,* starring John Wayne. Andy Devine drove the stage and shouted encouragement to the horses. There were three hitches of six horses each used on the stagecoach route.

123. BILLY—Philip Astley's first performing horse. Astley's late-18th-century shows were the first modern circuses.

124. BILLY—One of Union General George Thomas's war-horses in the Civil War, a big, powerful but steady and deliberate bay horse named after William T. Sherman.

125. BILLY—A dark bay stallion, the legendary sire of the American Quarter Horse around the time of the Civil War.

126. BILLY—Union Colonel James Penfield's war-horse in the Civil War. The Morgan survived the war and died of old age. His name is on a stone shaft in New York state commemorating the men of Company H and their horses.

127. BILLY—One of Union Lieutenant Frank Haskell's warhorses in the Civil War. Despite a wound in his lung that Haskell was unaware of, BILLY carried Haskell back to camp after the fighting before he died.

128. BILLY—Sculptor Thomas Eakins' horse, used as a model for an equestrian statue of Lincoln.

129. BILLY—One of the horses that William F. ("Buffalo Bill") Cody rode in his Wild West shows. Billy died at sea returning from a European tour.

130. BILLY BARTON—A rogue racehorse that was ruled off the flat track and went on to win the Maryland Hunt Cup in 1926. He almost won the 1928 Grand National Steeplechase but stumbled at the last fence and lost to long-shot TIPPERARY TIM. He came in second in that race, and those two were the only finishers out of 42 starters.

Birdwell, Jess—see LADY, RED ROVER.

THE BISCUIT—see SEABISCUIT.

THE BLACK—see THE BLACK STALLION.

131. BLACK ALLAN—The foundation sire of the Tennessee Walking Horse that was foaled in 1886 and failed as both a pacer and a trotter because of his unusually loose stride. He was owned by E.D. Herr of Lexington, Kentucky. At age 17, he was purchased by James Brantly, who bred him to a Walking mare named Gertrude. BLACK ALLAN became recognized as the foundation sire of the breed in 1935. He is also called ALLAN F-1.

132. BLACK BEAUTY—Art Acord's horse in western movies.

133. BLACK BEAUTY—The black horse in the Anna Sewell's 1877 book *Black Beauty*. The book was written to protest cruel treatment of carriage horses.

    Black Beauty, book—see BLACK BEAUTY (133), CAPTAIN (231), DUCHESS, GINGER, MERRYLEGS, PET, ROB ROY.

    Black Beauty, movie—see FURY (466).

134. BLACK BESS—One of Confederate General John Hunt Morgan's horses in the Civil War, a black mare.

135. BLACK BESS—A small black Anglo-Arabian mare ridden by Dick Turpin, a British highwayman hanged in 1739. His story is told in William Harrison Ainsworth's novel, *Rookwood*, in which a fictional 200-mile ride from London to York kills BLACK BESS.

136. BLACK COMET—A racing pony in the book *Misty of Chincoteague* by Marguerite Henry.

    Black Cyclone, movie—see REX (973).

    BLACK DENMARK—see GAINES DENMARK.

137. BLACK DIAMOND—The black American Saddle Horse that took MISTY's place as top movie horse after MISTY's death. He appeared in *The Flame of Araby* (1951) and *The Track of the Cat* (1954).

138. BLACK GOLD—The 1924 Kentucky Derby winner, a black colt, believed to be jinxed because he later broke a leg during a race and had to be destroyed.

139. BLACK HAWK—A well-known trotting horse; also the name of a line of trotters that were in their prime in the 1850s and preceded the Hambletonian horses.

    "Black Horses"—see FOFO.

140. BLACK JACK—The big black Thoroughbred with a star on its forehead that was a ceremonial horse for the United States Army. He was never ridden but was led riderless in many funeral processions, including those of Herbert Hoover, John F. Kennedy, Douglas MacArthur, and Lyndon B. Johnson. BLACK JACK died at the age of 29.

141. BLACK JACK—Union General John Logan's war-horse, killed by Logan's enemies.

142. BLACK KETTLE—A Kentucky Thoroughbred lost from a Mormon pioneer wagon train when Indians attacked them.

143. BLACK NELL—One of James Butler ("Wild Bill") Hickok's horses, a mare that died in 1870.

144. THE BLACK OF SAINGLEND—A magic horse belonging to Cuchulainn in Celtic legend. When Cuchulainn, the Irish Achilles, was born, a mare foaled at the same time and the two foals she had were given to him. SAINGLEND is also spelled SAINGLAIN. The other's name was THE GRAY OF MACHA.

145. THE BLACK STALLION—The black Arabian stallion in the Walter Farley series of stories including *The Black Stallion* and *The Black Stallion Returns*. Also known as THE BLACK, he was trained by Alec Ramsey to be a racehorse. THE BLACK STALLION was played by the black Arabian stallion CASS OLE in the 1979 movie, *The Black Stallion* and in the 1983 movie *The Black Stallion Returns*.

   The Black Stallion and *The Black Stallion Returns,* books and movies—see THE BLACK STALLION, CASS OLE, MIDNIGHT (766), NAPOLEON (806).

146. BLACK TOM—The tall black Thoroughbred charger Charles May rode in the Mexican War. When BLACK

TOM died, his four hooves were made into drinking cups.

BLACK WHIRLWIND—see DOMINO (363).

Blackford, Colonel—see COMET (283).

147. BLACKIE—One of the horses that pulled the Overland Stage in the 1939 movie, *Stagecoach,* starring John Wayne. Andy Devine drove the stage and shouted encouragement to the horses. There were three hitches of six horses each used on the stagecoach route.

148. BLACKIE—Chief Sitting Bull's black war-horse in the 1850s.

149. BLACKJACK—Allan ("Rocky") Lane's horse in western movies.

Blackmore, R.D., author—see KICKUMS, WINNIE.

150. BLANCHARD—Charlemagne's favorite charger in Carolingian legend.

151. BLANK—Cinderella's mare in one version of the tale. Name means "white" and "loss of memory."

152. BLARNEY—The wagon-train master Callahan's horse in the 1973 television show, "Dusty's Trail."

153. BLAUNCHKYNG—The gray Irish gelding that Laurence Olivier rode in the 1944 movie, *Henry V.*

154. BLAZE—Billy's pony in C.W. Anderson's books about Billy and BLAZE.

BLAZE KING—see KING (631).

155. BLEISTEIN—President Theodore Roosevelt's favorite horse while in the White House, a horse with a docked tail.

156. BLIND TOM—A blind gelding that pulled flatcars for the Union Pacific Railroad around 1866.

157. BLODIGHOFI—One of Frey's horses in Nordic mythology.

158. BLOOSOM—Gabby Hayes' mule in movies.

159. BLOSSOM—Tumbleweed's horse in Tom Ryan's comic strip, "Tumbleweeds."

160. BLUE—Curly's horse in the 1955 movie, *Oklahoma!*

161. BLUE BOY—Mark McCain's horse in the television show, "The Rifleman."

162. BLUESKIN—One of George Washington's horses on the census listing his animals in 1785. Washington had used the horse as a war charger, but BLUESKIN did not do well in battle.

163. BO—Rooster Cogburn's horse in Charles Portis's book, *True Grit*. The horse's name was BEAU in the 1969 movie *True Grit*.

164. BOB—President Abraham Lincoln's horse while in office. Also called ROBIN.

Bojer, Johan, author—see SKOBELEF.

165. BOLD ARRANGEMENT—The horse that came in second in the 1986 Kentucky Derby. He was fed one pint of Guinness stout daily with his oats and carrots.

166. BOLD FORBES—The 1976 Kentucky Derby winner, a small (15.2-hand) black colt that won wire to wire. He was found to be treated with Butazolidin, which had been legalized.

167. BOLD RULER—Thoroughbred racehorse named Horse of the Year in 1957. He was the sire of the 1973

Triple Crown winner SECRETARIAT. BOLD RULER died in 1971.

168. **BOLD VENTURE**—The 1936 Kentucky Derby winner, a chestnut colt.

Boldt, Harry—see WOYCHECK.

"Bonanza," television show—see BEAUTY (101), BUCK (199), CHUB, COCHISE.

Bonaparte, Napoleon—see ALI, AUSTERLITZ, COCO (272), DESIREE, JAFFA, MARENGO, MARIE, ROITELET, VIZIR, WAGRAM.

BONES—see EXTERMINATOR.

Bonner, Vint—see SCAR (1038).

169. **BONNIE**—One of the horses that pulled the Overland Stage in the 1939 movie, *Stagecoach,* starring John Wayne. Andy Devine drove the stage and shouted encouragement to the horses. There were three hitches of six horses each used on the stagecoach route.

170. **BONNIE SCOTLAND**—An English stallion that was a foundation sire for the American Quarter Horse.

The Book of Kings—see RAKSH.

The Book of Wonder—see SHEPPERALK.

171. **BOOMER**—A white Shetland pony that was the mascot, along with SOONER, of the University of Oklahoma's football team, the Sooners, in the 1970s. The two ponies pulled a small covered wagon around the goalposts after touchdowns.

172. **BOOMERANG**—One of Eddie Macken's famous show jumpers.

Boone, Elizabeth—see COED COCH BUDDAI.

Boone, Richard—see RAFTER.

Booth, John Wilkes—see COLA, UNKNOWN HORSE (1240).

Booth, Junius Brutus—see PEACOCK.

173. BOOTLEGGER—One of roper, actor, and entertainer Will Rogers' polo ponies, a black horse foaled in 1916.

174. BOOTS—A gelding that starred in movies and portrayed a wild horse in *The Misfits* with Clark Gable.

BORAK—see AL BORAK.

BORN FREE—see MR. RYTHM.

Boulanger, General Georges—see TUNIS.

175. BOURBON KING—A well-known American Saddle Horse descended from TOM HAL.

176. BOXER—The 18-hand cart horse in George Orwell's book, *Animal Farm,* that accepted the leadership of Napoleon the boar. When this hardworking horse was ready to retire, the pigs sent him to the knackers, while telling the other animals that he was going to the hospital.

Boyd, William—see TOPPER.

Boys' Life, magazine—see PEDRO.

177. BR FEROUK ROBERT—Patrick Swayze's Western Pleasure Arabian gelding in 1988.

Brand—see FREYFAX.

178. BRANDY—Clint Walker's horse's real name in the television show, "Cheyenne."

Brantly, James—see BLACK ALLAN.

179. BREE—The wise talking horse in C.S. Lewis's book *The Horse and His Boy,* the fifth book in the series *The Chronicles of Narnia.* Name means "prideful."

180. BRET HANOVER—An ideal Standardbred and well-known pacer from the 1960s.

181. BRIDESMAID—One of the horses that pulled the Overland Stage in the 1939 movie, *Stagecoach,* starring John Wayne. Andy Devine drove the stage and shouted encouragement to the horses. There were three hitches of six horses each used on the stagecoach route.

182. BRIGADORE—Sir Guyon's horse in Edmund Spenser's book *The Faerie Queene.* BRIGADORE had a horseshoe-shaped black mark in his mouth. Name means "bridle." Also spelled BRIGLIADORE.

183. BRIGHAM—An Indian pony ridden by William F. ("Buffalo Bill") Cody that earned him the title of Buffalo Bill. BRIGHAM was named after the Mormon leader Brigham Young; while he was an unattractive horse, he was fast and had been trained for buffalo chasing. BRIGHAM would race alongside the buffalo long enough for Cody to shoot at them, then would turn away. He helped Cody bring down over four thousand buffalo in seventeen months.

184. BRIGHTY—The wild burro in Marguerite Henry's book *Brighty of the Grand Canyon.*

BRIGLIADORE—see BRIGADORE.

185. BRIGLIADORO—Orlando's great steed in Carolingian legend.

Brimley, Wilford—see SNOWFLAKE (1100).

186. BROADWAY JOE—Bing Crosby's racehorse in the 1950 movie, *Riding High.*

187. THE BROGUE—The brown hunter gelding in *Beasts and Super-Beasts,* by Saki (H.H. Munro).

188. BROIEFORT—The black Arabian with a white star and stockinged forelegs ridden into battle by Ogier, the Dane in Danish legend. Also spelled BEIFFROR and BROIFFORT. BROIEFORT died in battle.

"Broken Arrow," television show—see SHEIK.

189. BROKERS TIP—The 1933 Kentucky Derby winner, a brown colt. That was the only race he ever won.

Brolin, James—see LAD'S VANDY.

190. BRONTE—One of the horses belonging to Helios, the sun god in classical mythology.

Bronte, Charlotte, author—see MESROUR.

191. BROOKLYN SUPREME—A Belgian draft stallion that weighed 3,200 pounds, stood 19.2 hands, lived between 1928 and 1948, and was considered to be the heaviest horse in history. He was not the tallest horse, however.

Broome, David—see RED A.

BROWN BEAUTY—see UNKNOWN HORSE (1225).

Brown, Johnny Mack—see REBEL.

192. BROWN ROAN—A horse ridden by Confederate General Robert E. Lee early in the Civil War that was not up to the strain of battle.

Brown, Sarah—see ARIZONA PIE.

Brown, Velvet—see ARIZONA PIE, KING (631), THE PIE (907).

193. BROWNIE—Bob Steele's horse in early western movies.

Browning, Robert, author—see ROLAND.

194. BRUIN—Sam Houston's chestnut mule in the mid-1800s.

Brunhild—see VINGSKORNIR.

Brunhilde—see GRANI.

195. BUBBLING OVER—The 1926 Kentucky Derby winner, a chestnut colt.

196. BUCEPHALUS—The favorite mount of Alexander the Great, a black stallion with a white triangle on his forehead that resembled an ox head. BUCEPHALUS means "ox head." Young Alexander tamed the horse and rode him in all his conquests. He founded the city of Bucephala around 326 B.C., named in honor of BUCEPHALUS, after the horse died of a war injury at that site. The horse was buried in an alabaster tomb. Alexander the Great died two years later.

197. BUCHANAN—The 1884 Kentucky Derby winner, a chestnut colt. The Derby was his first race.

198. BUCK—One of the Budweiser Clydesdale geldings from the eight-horse hitch that toured the fourteen western states.

199. BUCK—Ben Cartwright's buckskin gelding in the television show, "Bonanza," 1959–1973.

BUCK—see MARSHAL.

200. BUCKPASSER—A great racehorse that was named Horse of the Year in 1966.

201. BUCKSHOT—James Butler ("Wild Bill") Hickok's horse in real life and in the television show "Wild Bill Hickok," 1952–1958. Hickok was a U.S. Marshal.

202. BUCKSKIN JOE—A large yellow horse that William F. ("Buffalo Bill") Cody rode during his early scouting and hunting trips. Cody won the Congressional Medal of Honor after an Indian fight in which he rode BUCK-SKIN JOE. BUCKSKIN JOE was retired after he went blind following a 195-mile ride in which Cody escaped from pursuing Indians. BUCKSKIN JOE died in 1882 of old age.

Buddha—see KANTHAKA, LAMPON.

Budweiser Clydesdales—see ANDY, BARON REAL-IZATION, BILL (121), BUCK (198), CAPTAIN (232), COMMANDER, DEAN, DUKE (380), JAKE, MARK, SAMMY.

Buffalo Bill—see BILLY (129), BRIGHAM, BUCK-SKIN JOE, GRAY GHOST, ISHAM, MCKINLEY, MUSON, OLD CHARLIE, OLD SMOKY, PRINCE, SOLDIER BOY, TALL BULL.

Buffalo Bill, movie—see STEEL.

203. BULLE ROCK—The first Thoroughbred imported to the United States from England, in 1730 at the age of 21.

204. BULLET—A bay horse used by Confederate General Jeb Stuart during the Civil War.

205. BULRUSH—One of Justin Morgan's sons, he helped establish the Morgan horse breed. Also called THE BULRUSH MORGAN.

Bunbury, Sir Charles—see DIOMED.

206. BURGOO KING—The 1932 Kentucky Derby winner, a chestnut colt.

Burk, Clyde—see BALDY (79).

207. BURMESE—One of Queen Elizabeth II's ceremonial mounts, a black mare that she rode in the 1970s. The mare was given to her by the Royal Canadian Mounted Police.

208. BURNS—Union General George B. McClellan's tall black horse during the Civil War. The horse would wheel in the midst of battle to head back to the stable when it was time for dinner. McClellan developed the McClellan military saddle.

Burns, Robert, poet—see JENNY GEDDES, MAGGIE (715, 716).

Burnside, Ambrose—see DICK (348), MAJOR (724).

209. BUSHER—A well-known racehorse, a filly.

210. BUSSACO—A sweet-natured chestnut Lusitano stallion given to Queen Elizabeth II by the president of Portugal. The stallion was often loaned out to guests in the 1950s.

Butch Cassidy and the Sundance Kid, movie—see HUD.

211. BUTLER—One of Confederate General Wade Hampton's war-horses in the Civil War. The bay, presented to him by Colonel Butler, was a good jumper and won a jumping contest after the war against Union General Kilpatrick's Arabian OLD SPOT.

Butler, General Benjamin—see EBONY, WARREN.

Butler, Daws—see QUICK DRAW MCGRAW.

Butler, Rhett—see MARSE ROBERT.

212. BUTTERCUP—One of Annie Oakley's horses in the television show, "Annie Oakley," 1953–1958.

213. BUTTERMILK—The buckskin gelding owned by Dale Evans and ridden by her in the television show, "The Roy Rogers Show," 1951–1964.

214. BUTTERMILK—Joe Riley's horse in the television show, "Laredo."

215. BUTTON—Horse belonging to Revolutionary American political writer Thomas Paine.

216. BYERLY TURK—The first of three Arabian stallions imported to England to found the breed of horses known as the English Thoroughbred. Foaled in 1679, and taken as a spoil of war by Captain Byerly in 1686 in a Turkish war, the horse was sent to England in 1689. He is the great-great grandsire of HEROD. The other two stallions were THE DARLEY ARABIAN and THE GODOLPHIN BARB.

Byrne, Donn, author—see DUCKS AND DRAKES, LIMIRICK PRIDE.

217. CABALL—One of the horses belonging to the legendary King Arthur.

218. CACAO—One of the two horses kept by Agent James T. West in the television show "Wild Wild West." They were kept in a special railroad car.

219. CACTUS—Reese Bennett's horse in the television show, "Laredo."

220. CACTUS KATE—A movie mare ridden by William S. Hart. The mare was devoted to Hart's horse FRITZ.

221. CAESAR—The horse in the story, *Ben: Story of a Cart Horse*.

222. CAESAR—Union Captain Frederick Otto Fritsch's bay war-horse in the Civil War. Between battles, CAESAR was shown in a review for President Lincoln in which he won a horse race and jumped a 5-foot fence with a 9-foot ditch beyond it.

Calamity Jane, movie—see DOLLAR (357).

Calhoun, Ben—see HANNIBAL.

Calhoun, Rory—see DOMINO (360).

223. CALICO—One of Gabby Hayes's horses in western movies.

Caligula, Roman emperor—see INCITATUS.

Callahan, Mr.—see BLARNEY.

224. CALLIOPE—A 3-year-old chestnut filly in John Galsworthy's, *Caravan: the Assembled Tales of John Galsworthy*. The story "Had a Horse" is about CALLIOPE and three other racehorses.

Calumet Farm—see CITATION, WHIRLAWAY.

Cameron, Rod—see KNIGHT.

Campbell, Glen—see JUNIOR.

Campbell, J.E.—see PAL (870).

"Camptown Races," song—see FLORA TEMPLE.

225. CANDY—Hugh O'Brian's horse's real name in the television show, "The Life and Times of Wyatt Earp."

226. CANDY BOY—A 15.2-hand bay cutting horse from Wyoming that Tommy Smith rode as a child. He said he learned balance, grip, and rhythm from the horse. Smith went on to win the 1965 Grand National Steeplechase on JAY TRUMP.

227. CANNON BALL—The foundation sire of the Irish Connemara pony breed.

228. CANNONADE—The 1974 Kentucky Derby winner, a bay colt.

229. CANONERO II—The 1971 Kentucky Derby winner, a bay colt with an unremarkable pedigree. He was foaled in Kentucky in 1968, but was sent to Venezuela to be trained and to race. The Derby was his first race in America, and when he came from behind to win it there were no Spanish interpreters available to interview his trainer. He also won the Preakness wire to wire. He ran in the Belmont with an infected leg and came in fourth. His original price had been $1,200; when he went to stud it was $1 million.

230. CAPILET—Sir Andrew Aguecheek's gray horse in William Shakespeare's play, *Twelfth Night*.

231. CAPTAIN—The old war-horse in Anna Sewell's book, *Black Beauty,* which describes his experiences in the Battle of Balaklava as part of the British Light Brigade.

232. CAPTAIN—One of the Budweiser Clydesdale geldings in the eight-horse hitch that toured the fourteen western states.

233. THE CAPTAIN—The horse in the animated movie, *101 Dalmations.*

Caravan, book—see CALLIOPE, HANGMAN, PARROT, THE SHIRKER.

Cardigan, 7th earl of—see RONALD.

234. CARDIGAN BAY—A well-known pacer gelding from New Zealand in the 1950s and 1960s that became harness racing's first millionaire in the late 1960s. The horse retired at the age of 12 in 1968.

235. CARIOCA II—A successful dressage horse ridden by Dominique d'Esme.

236. CARLOS—Don Hernando de Soto's 17-hand horse, which he took to Cuba and Florida in the 1500s.

Carradine, David—see INDIAN WOMAN.

Carrillo, Leo—see CONQUISTADOR (287), LOCO.

237. CARROT—A 14-hand sorrel stallion rope horse in the 1940s that was used in calf roping and team roping. He sired many good cow horses that were fast and gentle. He died in 1955.

238. CARRY BACK—The 1961 Kentucky Derby winner, a brown colt with an unremarkable pedigree that was called THE PEOPLE'S HORSE.

Carson, Kit—see APACHE (49).

Carson, Sunset—see SILVER (1070).

Cartwright, Adam—see BEAUTY (101).

Cartwright, Ben—see BUCK (199).

Cartwright, Hoss—see CHUB.

Cartwright, Little Joe—see COCHISE.

Carver, Sonora—see DUCHESS OF LIGHTNING, JOHN THE BAPTIST, JUDAS, KLATAWAH,

POWDER FACE (926), RED LIPS, SILVER KING (1078), SNOW.

239. CASEY'S SHADOW—The star of the 1978 family movie, *Casey's Shadow*, about Quarter Horse racing.

"Casper, the Friendly Ghost," television show—see NIGHTMARE.

240. CASS OLE—The black Arabian stallion that starred in the 1979 movie, *The Black Stallion* and the 1983 movie, *The Black Stallion Returns*, based on the books by Walter Farley. CASS OLE was a show horse and had four white stockings and a white star before being dyed and trained for the movies by Glenn and Corky Randall.

Castor and Pollux—see CYLLAROS.

Cat Ballou, movie—see SMOKEY.

241. CATALINA—A sorrel Arabian owned by President Ronald Reagan.

Catlin, George—see CHARLEY (254).

242. CAVALCADE—The 1934 Kentucky Derby winner, a brown colt.

243. CENTENNIAL—A big black gelding ridden by Queen Elizabeth II in ceremonial parades in the 1970s.

244. CERUS—Horse that, along with ARION, pulled a chariot for Adrastus in Greek mythology.

Cervantes (Saavedra, Miguel de), author—see CLAVILENO, DAPPLE, ROSINANTE.

Chacaro, Wild Pony of the Pampas—see GITANA, OSOSO.

245. CHAMP—A Belgian horse that starred, along with RUBE, in the film *Chester, Yesterday's Horse.*

246. CHAMP VI—A bay pony stallion ridden by Debbie Johnsey in the British Junior Show Jumping Team, and later ridden by Clair Johnsey.

247. CHAMPION—Gene Autry's palomino horse that starred in western movies and in the 1950 television show "The Gene Autry Show," and in the 1950s television show "The Adventures of Champion," which also starred 12-year-old Ricky North. CHAMPION was called the "World's Wonder Horse" and his hoofprints are in front of Grauman's Chinese Theater in Hollywood. One of the horses that played CHAMPION was a chestnut Tennessee Walker that was originally called LINDY because he was foaled on the day Lindbergh made his New York to Paris flight in 1927.

Champion, Bob—see ALDANITI.

248. CHANCE SHOT—A Thoroughbred racehorse from the FAIR PLAY line that influenced the running Quarter Horse in the late 1920s.

249. CHANCELLOR—One of the horses ridden by Confederate General Jeb Stuart during the Civil War. The horse was killed during the Battle of Chancellorsville.

250. CHANT—The 1894 Kentucky Derby winner, a bay colt owned by the famous Dodge City Deputy Sheriff Bill Tilghman.

251. CHAPEL—One of roper, actor, and entertainer Will Rogers' horses, a bay that he rode in dangerous movie scenes.

The Charge of the Light Brigade, movie—see RONALD.

252. CHARISMA—The Olympic Three-Day Event horse that was ridden to gold medal victory in Los Angeles and that won the individual gold medal with New Zealander Mark Todd as his rider at Seoul in 1988. CHARISMA retired after that win.

253. CHARITY—A mare that won the Grand National Steeplechase in 1841, the first mare to win that race.

Charlemagne, King—see BLANCHARD, TENCENDUR.

Charles, Prince—see BANDIT, SAN QUININA, SOMBRA.

Charles II, King of England—see OLD ROWLEY.

Charles III, King of Spain—see ROYAL GIFT.

Charles VIII, King of France—see SAVOY.

254. CHARLEY—The claybank pony that George Catlin rode for 500 miles while studying and painting the North American Indians.

255. CHARLEY—Confederate guerrilla leader William Clarke Quantrill's horse in the Civil War.

256. CHARLIE—One of Union General Nathaniel Banks' war-horses in the Civil War. He loaned the horse to General Ulysses S. Grant in 1863, and Grant had an impromptu race against another officer. A train startled CHARLIE during the race and he swerved suddenly, unseating and wounding Grant, who was then out of action for several months. CHARLIE was not blamed for Grant's injuries but became known as the only horse to unseat the general.

CHARLIE—see OLD CHARLIE.

257. CHARRO—A wild horse that traveled with the Thoroughbred horse COLONEL in Will James' book, *The Dark Horse.*

258. CHATEAUGAY—The 1963 Kentucky Derby winner, a chestnut colt.

Chatelet, Madame—see HIRONDELLE, ROSSIGNOL.

Chester, Yesterday's Horse, movie—see CHAMP, RUBE.

"Cheyenne," television show—see BRANDY.

259. CHICA D'ORO—Linda Craig's palomino filly in the mystery stories by Ann Sheldon.

260. CHICKO—A burro in *Little Don Pedro,* by Helen Holland Graham.

261. CHIEF—The last cavalry horse on the U.S. government payroll; foaled in 1932 and retired in 1958.

262. CHILE—One of the horses that pulled the Overland Stage in the 1939 movie, *Stagecoach,* starring John Wayne and Andy Devine. There were three six-horse hitches used on their Arizona run. Andy Devine was the driver who shouted encouragement to the horses.

The Chimera—see PEGASUS (886).

THE CHOCOLATE SOLDIER—see EQUIPOISE.

The Chronicles of Narnia, books—see BREE, FLEDGE, HWIN, STRAWBERRY.

263. CHUB—Hoss Cartwright's dark brown horse on the television show "Bonanza," 1959–1973.

Churchill, Winston—see ARAB, TRAVELLER (1204).

264. CINCINNATI—The 17-hand dark bay Saddle Horse–type charger that carried Union General Ulysses S. Grant during the Civil War. Also spelled CINCINNATUS. He was a gift to Grant from a dying man in Cincinnati, Ohio. CINCINNATI was the son of Lexington, a Thoroughbred racer, and Grant once refused $10,000 in gold for him. President Lincoln once rode him. After the war CINCINNATI retired to the farm and died in 1878.

Cinderella—see BLANK, MAJOR (723).

"The Cisco Kid," television show—see DIABLO, LOCO.

265. CITATION—A great Thoroughbred racehorse owned and bred by Calumet Farm. The bay colt, also known as BIG CY, was the winner of the Triple Crown in 1948. His jockey, Eddie Arcaro, who won the Kentucky Derby five times, said that riding him was like riding in a Cadillac. In 1951 he became the first Thoroughbred horse to win $1 million. He retired the same year. CITATION died in 1970 at the age of 25.

266. CLAVILENO—The magical wooden horse ridden by Don Quixote in Part 2 of Cervantes' book *Don Quixote*. Name means "wooden peg." Also called ALIGERO CLAVILENO.

CLEVER HANS—see KLUGE HANS.

CLEVER JACK—see KLUGE HANS.

Clewes, Dorothy, author—see LITTLE WHITE STAR.

Clint—see SMOKY.

267. CLOVER—The stout, motherly mare and cart horse in George Orwell's book *Animal Farm* that accepted the leadership of the boar Napoleon.

THE CLUB-FOOTED COMET—see ASSAULT.

268. CLYDE VAN DUSEN—The 1929 Kentucky Derby winner, a chestnut gelding, whose trainer's name was also Clyde Van Dusen.

Coakes, Marion—see STROLLER.

Coates Family—see JUMPER.

Coble, John C.—see STEAMBOAT (1124).

269. COCHISE—Little Joe Cartwright's black-and-white paint horse on the television show "Bonanza," 1959–1973.

270. COCKATOO—The horse in *Phillipa's Fox Hunt* by Edith Somerville and Martin Ross.

271. COCO—Nick Barkley's horse in the television show, "The Big Valley."

272. COCO—One of Napoleon Bonaparte's many horses, a cream-colored Norman that he rode in ceremonies and parades.

Cody, Bill—see KING (634).

Cody, William F. ("Buffalo Bill")—see BILLY (129), BRIGHAM, BUCKSKIN JOE, GRAY GHOST, ISHAM, MCKINLEY, MUSON, OLD CHARLIE, OLD SMOKY, PRINCE, SOLDIER BOY, TALL BULL.

273. COED COCH BUDDAI—A 12.2-hand, dapple-gray Welsh pony ridden by Elizabeth Boone in the British Pony Club.

274. COLA—The pet horse belonging to John Wilkes Booth when the assassin was a child. He taught the black colt to do many tricks.

275. COLD DECK—A legendary sire of the American Quarter Horse, a dark sorrel, foaled in 1862.

276. COLONEL—The Thoroughbred horse that traveled with the wild horse CHARRO in Will James' book, *Dark Horse*.

277. THE COLONEL—The winner of the Grand National Steeplechase in 1869 and 1870, the second horse to win in successive years.

278. COLONEL MERRYBOY—Tennis star Maureen Connolly's Tennessee Walker in the 1950s. A riding accident on the horse ended Connolly's tennis career in 1954.

279. COLUMBUS—A big gray horse ridden by Princess Anne in the 1970s and later by her husband, Mark Phillips.

280. COMANCHE—The dun-colored war-horse of Captain Myles Keogh named after the Comanche arrow that wounded him in his first military action. He was also one of the survivors of Custer's Last Stand against Sioux warriors at the Battle of the Little Big Horn in Montana in 1876. COMANCHE was nursed back to health and kept by the 7th Cavalry for use in parades and ceremonies. He was given a bucket of beer on payday and died of colic in 1891. His body was mounted and put on exhibit at the Museum of the University of Kansas in Lawrence.

281. COMANCHE—One of roper, actor, and entertainer Will Rogers' horses, a cream-colored horse that Rogers rode in Wild West shows.

Come On, Seabiscuit, book—see SEABISCUIT.

282. COMET—The superhorse that Supergirl rides in the Supergirl comic books.

283. COMET—Confederate Colonel Blackford's dark mahogany bay horse during the Civil War. COMET had a white star.

284. COMMANDER—One of the Budweiser Clydesdale geldings from the eight-horse hitch that toured the fourteen western states.

285. CONDE—Frederick the Great of Prussia's favorite horse, in the late 1700s, a piebald gelding. CONDE died at age 38 in 1804.

Connolly, Maureen—see COLONEL MERRYBOY.

Connors, Chuck—see RAZOR.

Conqueror, movie—see STEEL (1127).

286. CONQUISTADOR—Pablito's horse in the Disney movie, *The Littlest Outlaw.*

287. CONQUISTADOR—Leo Carrillo's palomino horse in early western movies.

288. CONVERSANO—One of the founding sires of the famous Lippizan horses of the Spanish Riding School.

Cooper, Gary—see FLASH (438).

289. COPENHAGEN—The favorite mount of the Duke of Wellington (Arthur Wellesley, also known as the Iron Duke), foaled in 1808. COPENHAGEN's grandsire was ECLIPSE. The chestnut war-horse was the stallion the Iron Duke rode to victory in the Battle of Waterloo in 1815. COPENHAGEN was spirited, prone to kick, and he liked to eat chocolate. He died in 1836 at age 28.

290. COPPER—Singing cowboy Eddie Dean's palomino horse in western movies.

291. COPPERBOTTOM—One of the foundation sires of the American Quarter Horse breed. He lived in the 1840s and was imported to Texas from Pennsylvania. He was a strain of the JANUS line and a grandson of DIOMED.

292. CORKRAN OF CLAMSTRETCH—The racehorse hero of "Corkran of Clamstretch," by John Biggs, Jr.

293. CORNCRACKER—Young Dick Handley's black colt in the 1950 movie *The Asphalt Jungle*.

294. CORNPLANTER—A circus horse ridden by John Bill Ricketts in 1793. Rickett's circus, the first true circus in America, burned down in 1799. CORNPLANTER jumped over other horses, including SILVA, a horse of his own height, and Ricketts did trick riding on him. Ricketts also bought George Washington's old horse JACK for a sideshow.

Cortes, Hernando—see EL MORZILLO.

295. COSA RARA—King Ludwig II of Bavaria's favorite gray mare that he once fed indoors off his good china.

296. COSSACK—A favorite dun-colored horse ridden by Queen Elizabeth II in the 1970s.

297. COUNT FLEET—The 1943 Triple Crown winner, a small, 15.2-hand brown colt, also known as THE COUNT and THE FLEET. His sire was REIGH COUNT, the 1928 Kentucky Derby winner, and COUNT FLEET sired the 1951 Kentucky Derby winner, COUNT TURF. COUNT FLEET won wire to wire in the Kentucky Derby and was named Horse of the Year in 1943. When he retired to stud he became a leading sire and was stabled with the stallion NEVELE

PRIDE, a Standardbred that was devoted to him. He died in 1973 at age 33.

298. COUNT TURF—The 1951 Kentucky Derby winner, a bay colt, sired by COUNT FLEET.

299. COUNTERPOINT—A well-known chestnut race-horse.

300. COUNTRY GENTLEMAN—The horse that starred in the movie *Smoky*.

301. COWBOY—One of roper, actor, and entertainer Will Rogers' horses, a one-eyed sorrel that Rogers used in roping performances.

302. COWBOY JOE and COWBOY JOE II—Pinto Shet-land-Welsh cross ponies that were mascots for the University of Wyoming Cowboys football team. The first COWBOY JOE started in the early 1950s and COWBOY JOE II was the mascot in the 1970s.

Crabbe, Buster—see FALCON.

Crane, Ichabod—see GUNPOWDER.

Crawford, Joan—see BEAUTY (102).

303. CREOLE—A horse ridden by Robert E. Lee in the Mexican War.

304. THE CRISP HORSE—A Suffolk mare in 1768 belong-ing to Mr. Crisp of Ufford, Sussex. All Suffolk horses trace back to this mare.

305. CRISTOBALITO—The palomino Paso Fino stallion in the 1970 Disney TV movie, *Cristobalito, the Calypso Colt*.

Crosby, Bing—see BROADWAY JOE, ZOMBIE.

306. CRUISER—A savage, Thoroughbred that horse-tamer John Rarey was able to tame in the 1800s.

Crump, Diane—see FATHOM.

307. CRUSADER—A well-known chestnut racehorse sired by MAN O'WAR.

Crusades—see FAUVEL.

Cuchulainn—see THE BLACK OF SAINGLEND, THE GRAY OF MACHA.

308. CUCO BRITCHES—A horse from the television show "Gunsmoke."

Curly—see BLUE.

Curly, Crow scout—see UNKNOWN HORSE (1235).

Curly Top, movie—see SPUNKY.

309. CURTAL—A horse with a docked tail in William Shakespeare's play, *All's Well That Ends Well.*

Custer, George A.—see CUSTIS LEE, DANDY, DON JUAN (365), HARRY, JACK RUCKER, PHIL SHERIDAN, ROANOKE, VIC.

Custer's Last Stand—see COMANCHE (280), LITTLE SCOUT'S PAINT HORSE, VIC.

310. CUSTIS LEE—One of Union Captain George A. Custer's horses during the Civil War. The horse later became Mrs. Custer's favorite saddle horse. CUSTIS LEE died when George Custer accidently shot the horse when out buffalo hunting.

311. CUT—A horse in William Shakespeare's play, *Henry IV, Pt. I.*

312. CYLLAROS—Twins Castor and Pollux's black horse in classical mythology. Also spelled CYLLARUS.

313. CYRIL—J. Thaddeus Toad's horse and companion in Kenneth Grahame's book, *The Wind in the Willows*.

314. CYROCK—One of the horses said to belong to Jesse James during his outlaw days.

Dag—see SKINFAXI.

315. DAHLIA—A 3-year-old filly that won the 1973 Washington, D.C., International race, the first filly to do so.

316. DAHMA—One of the five gallant Arabian mares that passed the endurance test in Mecca in the 7th century and founded the most notable families of Arabian horses. All five are referred to as El-Khamsa ("the Five"), or Al Khamseh. DAHMA was a black mare, and her name means "dark one."

Dalton, Emmett—see KATIE, RED BUCK.

317. DAN—A horse belonging to outlaw Frank James, brother of Jesse James.

318. DAN PATCH—A well-known early-day pacer, a Standardbred owned by Will Savage that was foaled in 1896. He raced for 9 years and 30 times ran the mile in under 2 minutes. His record mile of 1:54.5 at age 9 stood for 33 years. DAN PATCH died July 11, 1916, and Will Savage died the next day. DAN PATCH was harness racing's first hero, and toys, washing machines, and children were named after him.

Dancer, Stanley—see NEVELE PRIDE.

319. DANCER'S IMAGE—Although all the record books list this gray colt as the winner of the 1968 Kentucky Derby, he was taken down from first place for drugs and

did not receive any money. The drug was Butazolidin, which was not legal that year. FORWARD PASS was declared the winner.

320. DANDY—A bay horse ridden by George A. Custer that was left with the supply wagons during Custer's Last Stand and sent home to Custer's father after the battle.

321. DANIEL BOONE—A Standardbred harness racer that was taken to Australia from America in 1869 to start the sport in that country.

322. DANIEL WEBSTER—Union General George B. McClellan's dark bay Thoroughbred horse during the Civil War. DANIEL WEBSTER stood 17-hands tall and died in 1879 at age 23.

323. DANSEUSE—Jacqueline Bouvier's favorite horse when she was young girl.

324. DAPPLE—Sancho Panza's donkey in Cervantes' book, *Don Quixote*.

325. DAPPLEGRIM—A huge dapple-gray horse in Norse folktales that helped his young owner win the hand of a princess.

326. DAREDEVIL—The mettlesome black horse ridden by the Headless Horseman in Washington Irving's story *The Legend of Sleepy Hollow*.

The Dark Horse, book—see CHARRO, COLONEL (276).

327. DARK STAR—The 1953 Kentucky Derby winner, a brown colt, who won that race ahead of NATIVE DANCER, and was the only horse ever to so do.

328. DARLEY ARABIAN—One of the three Arabians imported into England to be the foundation sires of the

English Thoroughbred. Thomas Darley, the English consul in Syria, traded a rifle for him in Aleppo in 1703. He was the great-great-grandsire of the English ECLIPSE. He was also the forefather of MESSENGER, who was a grandfather of HAMBLETONIAN 10, foundation sire of the Standardbred. The other two Arabians were THE BYERLY TURK and THE GODOLPHIN BARB.

329. D'ARTAGNAN'S HORSE—The 13-year-old yellow pony with a hairless tail that traveled with his head lower than his knees in Alexandre Dumas' book *The Three Musketeers.*

330. DAVID HARUM'S BALKY HORSE—The balky horse in Edward Noyes Wescott's book, *David Harum.*

David of Sassoun—see JALALI.

Davis, Jefferson—see KENTUCKY, TARTAR (1165).

Davis, Robbie—see DRUMS IN THE NIGHT.

A Day at the Races, movie—see HI HAT.

Day, Doris—see DOLLAR (357).

331. DAY STAR—The 1878 Kentucky Derby winner, a chestnut colt.

332. DEAN—One of the Budweiser Clydesdale geldings from the eight-horse hitch that toured the fourteen western states.

Dean, Eddie—see COPPER, FLASH (439), WHITE CLOUD (1270).

Death Valley Days, movie—see OLD BLUE (846).

333. DECATUR—Union General Philip Kearny's light bay horse during the Civil War. Kearny had lost an arm in

the Mexican War and rode in battle with the reins in his mouth. DECATUR died in battle.

334. DECIDEDLY—The 1962 Kentucky Derby winner, a gray colt. His jockey was Bill Hartack, who has ridden five Kentucky Derby winners.

335. DEIMOS—Ares'/Mars' horse in classical mythology. Name means "panic."

336. DEJADO—A black Andalusian stallion featured in photographer Robert Vavra's 1989 book *Vavra's Horses,* as one of the world's 10 most beautiful equines.

de la Vega, Don Diego—see PHANTOM (898), TORNADO.

de Leyer, Harry—see SNOWMAN.

Demeter—see ARION.

337. DENMARK—A brown Thoroughbred stallion, foaled in 1839, that became the foundation sire of the American Saddle Horse breed, selected by the breed's association. He was mated in 1851 with the STEVENSON MARE to start the breed.

Denver Broncos—see T.D.

Derby, Lord—see HYPERION.

338. DESIREE—A white Arabian mare ridden by Napoleon Bonaparte.

d'Esme, Dominique—see CARIOCA II.

de Soto, Don Hernando—see CARLOS.

Destiny Bay—see DUCKS AND DRAKES, LIMIRICK PRIDE.

339. DETERMINE—The 1954 Kentucky Derby winner, a gray colt.

Devereaux, Walter—see REX BEACH.

Devine, Andy—see BABY, BESSIE, BILL (122), BLACKIE (147), BONNIE, BRIDESMAID, CHILE, HONEY, QUEENIE (939), SWEETHEART.

340. DEVON LOCH—Ridden by jockey and author Dick Francis in the Grand National Steeplechase in 1956 and owned by the Queen Mother. DEVON LOCH was in first place after the last fence, with only 100 feet to go, when he leaped as if to jump another fence. There was not another fence, however, and he fell on his belly with all four legs extended. Neither horse nor jockey was hurt, and no one knows why it happened.

341. DEXTER—A famous Civil War–era trotter gelding whose body was a model for 19th-century weathervanes. He was once driven by Ulysses S. Grant, and he was the model for a Currier and Ives print.

342. DHULDUL—The horse ridden by Ali, the son-in-law of the Prophet Muhammad in the 7th century.

343. DIABLO—The pinto horse owned by the Cisco Kid and ridden in the 1951 television show, "The Cisco Kid."

344. DIAMOND—The cab horse in George MacDonald's book *At the Back of the North Wind*. Also called OLD DIAMOND.

DIAMOND DECORATOR—see TORNADO.

Diamond, Neil—see HEARTLIGHT NO. ONE.

345. DICE—A small pinto stallion movie horse that starred in *It Happened in Hollywood*, 1935; *Zorro Rides Again*,

1936; *Arizona,* 1940; *Duel In the Sun,* 1946; and *Thunderhoof,* 1948. He was also ridden by Gene Autry early in Autry's career. DICE was owned and trained by Ralph McCutcheon.

346. DICK—One of Union Lieutenant Frank Haskell's war-horses in the Civil War. DICK was very cool under fire; even when struck repeatedly by bullets and shells, he did not collapse and die until Haskell had dismounted after the charge and unsaddled him. Haskell died later in the war.

347. DICK—Union Lieutenant Robert Oliver's war-horse in the Civil War. Oliver's father rode DICK in Fourth of July parades after the war until DICK died in 1885 at age 33. His picture, hoof, and saddle were preserved in the Oswego Historical Society in New York.

348. DICK—Union General Ambrose Burnside's favorite driving horse in the Civil War.

349. DICK TURPIN—One of Confederate Henry Douglas's horses in the Civil War.

350. DICTATOR—The son of HAMBLETONIAN and the foundation sire of the Dictator line of pacers.

Dietrich, Marlene—see KING JOHN.

Dietrich von Bern—see FALKE.

Dillon, Matt—see MARSHAL.

351. DINAH THE MULE—The mule in the television show "Our Gang."

Diocles—see POMPEIANUS.

352. DIOMED—Winner of the first Derby at Epson Downs in England in 1780. Owned by Sir Charles Bunbury,

who tossed a coin with the earl of Derby to see who the race would be named after. Derby won. The chestnut horse was imported to Virginia in 1789 and influenced the American Saddle Horse breed.

Diomedes—see THE MARES OF DIOMEDES.

"Dirty Sally," television show—see WORTHLESS.

353. DISCOVERY—A successful chestnut racehorse.

354. DISPLAY—A well-known ill-tempered racehorse also known as THE IRON HORSE.

355. DOBBIN—The horse in William Shakespeare's play *The Merchant of Venice.*

356. DOBHAR—A steed from Irish legend that belonged to the King of Siogair and could run on land or sea.

The Doctor—see NOBS.

357. DOLLAR—Sorrel horse in the 1953 movie, *Calamity Jane* and ridden by Doris Day and Joel McCrea in other western movies.

DOLLAR—see BEAU.

358. DOLLY—Horse belonging to Union General William Tecumseh Sherman in the Civil War until it was stolen from him.

359. DOLLY—A chestnut mare ridden in battle by George Washington.

360. DOMINO—The real name of the horse Rory Calhoun rode in the television show "The Texan."

361. DOMINO—Jeff Miller's pet colt in the television show "Lassie."

362. DOMINO—A black-and-white stallion that resembled DICE and was ridden by Charlton Heston in the 1958 movie, *The Big Country.*

363. DOMINO—A racehorse that was a descendant of ECLIPSE. His nickname was BLACK WHIRLWIND, and his sire was HIMYAR.

364. DON JUAN—Pepe's white stallion in the 1960 movie, *Pepe.* The horse's real name was KING COTTON.

365. DON JUAN—Union Captain George A. Custer's dark bay stallion during the Civil War. Few soldiers rode stallions then but Custer liked to be different. The stallion won many races; when Custer rode him in the victory march after the war, he let the horse race down Pennsylvania Avenue as if he were running away.

Don Quixote, book—see CLAVILENO, DAPPLE, ROSINANTE.

366. DONAU—The 1910 Kentucky Derby winner, a bay colt.

367. DONERAIL—The 1913 Kentucky Derby winner, a bay colt that won against odds of 91 to 1.

Doolittle, Eliza—see DOVER.

368. DOPEY—The small coal-black horse that Will Rogers used for roping performances in the movie, *The Roping Fool.* DOPEY died in 1934.

369. DOT—Eleanor Roosevelt's riding horse in the late 1930s.

370. DOUBLET—The chestnut gelding Princess Anne rode when she was presented the trophy for the 1971 World Three-Day Event Championship by her mother, Queen

Elizabeth II. DOUBLET broke a leg in 1974 at age 11 and had to be put down.

Douglas, Henry—see ASHBY, DICK TURPIN, JEB STUART.

371. DOUTELLE—Horse that won the 1957 2000 Guineas Trial Stakes for Queen Elizabeth II, and was the last of her three consecutive winners.

Dove, Dr. Daniel—see NOBS.

372. DOVER—The racehorse that Eliza Doolittle cheers for at Ascot in the movie, *My Fair Lady*. Eliza cries, "Come on, DOVER, move your bloomin' ass!"

Doyle, Sir Arthur Conan, author—see SILVER BLAZE.

The Drifting Cowboy—see RAGTIME.

373. DRIFTWOOD—A bay stallion and top rope horse that sired other good rope horses in the 1940s and 1950s in California. He died in 1960.

374. DRINKER OF THE WIND—The horse in Carl Raswan's book *Drinkers of the Wind*. He was called SHURABAT AL-RIH which means "drinker of the wind."

375. DRUMS IN THE NIGHT—Thoroughbred racehorse ridden by Idaho jockey Robbie Davis in a race in New York in 1988. When racehorse MR. WALTER K stumbled in front of him and the jockey, Mike Venezia, was thrown, DRUMS IN THE NIGHT was too close to jump over him and his hooves struck Venezia's head, killing him. Davis was traumatized by the event and did not ride again for five months.

376. DU—Hero Kulhwch's horse in Welsh legend.

377. DUCHESS—Black Beauty's mother in Anna Sewell's book *Black Beauty*. She was also called PET.

378. DUCHESS OF LIGHTNING—A gentle dapple-gray mare used in a horse diving act in the 1920s with Sonora Carver. The horse dove with Sonora on her back from a 40-foot tower into an 11-foot tank of water. The brave horse drowned when she was taken to California to dive into the ocean.

379. DUCKS AND DRAKES—The horse in Donn Byrne's book *Destiny Bay*. The horse was by Drake's Drum out of Little Duck.

Dudley Do-Right—see STEED.

Duel in the Sun, movie—see DICE, MISTY (785).

380. DUKE—One of the Budweiser Clydesdale geldings from the eight-horse hitch that toured the fourteen western states.

381. DUKE—One of the two horses ridden by Agent James T. West in the television show "Wild Wild West." They were kept in a special railroad car.

382. DUKE—One of the horses ridden in western movies by Tim Holt.

383. THE DUKE—The winner of the first Grand National Steeplechase at Aintree, England, in 1837, ridden by Henry Potts. There were only four runners.

Dumas, Alexandre, author—see D'ARTAGNAN'S HORSE.

384. DUNDRUM—An Irish pony jumper ridden by Tommy Wade.

Dunsay, Lord, author—see SHEPPERALK.

The Durango Kid—see RAIDER (947).

Durer, Albrecht, painter—see THE GREAT HORSE.

385. DUST COMMANDER—The 1970 Kentucky Derby winner, a chestnut colt.

Dusty—see FRECKLES.

"Dusty's Trail," television show—see BLARNEY, FRECKLES.

386. DYNAMITE—The wild stallion that Spin and Marty try to capture in the Spin-and-Marty segments of the television show, "The Mickey Mouse Club."

387. EAGLE—One of President Thomas Jefferson's horses in the early 1800s, a spirited older horse.

Eakins, Thomas—see BILLY (128).

Earl of Derby—see DIOMED.

Earth's Children, book series—see RACER, WHINNEY.

388. EASTER HERO—An American-owned horse entered in the Grand National Steeplechase in 1929. He did not win but finished the race gamely after hitting the top rail of one of the fences and twisting a shoe.

389. EBENEZER—The colt that was given, along with LITTLE BUB, to Justin Morgan in repayment of a debt in Marguerite Henry's book *Justin Morgan Had a Horse.*

390. EBENEZER—Chief Joseph's war-horse in the late 1800s, a light roan Appaloosa with red spots; it was a good racehorse.

391. EBONY—President Abraham Lincoln rode this black stallion during a review of the troops in 1864. Some

artillery fire startled EBONY, who bolted. The stallion was eventually stopped by an orderly, and Lincoln was able to finish the review. EBONY had been loaned to him for the occasion by General Benjamin Butler.

392. THE EBONY HORSE—A mechanical flying horse from *The Arabian Nights,* whose story was told by Scheherazade. It was made of ebony and ivory.

393. ECLIPSE (AMERICAN)—A well-known racehorse, foaled in 1814, that was the grandson of MESSENGER and related to the English ECLIPSE. Forty thousand people watched him lose in a match race to SIR ARCHY at Union Race Course on Long Island in 1823. Also called AMERICAN ECLIPSE.

394. ECLIPSE (ENGLISH)—The great-great-grandson of THE DARLEY ARABIAN, foaled April 1, 1764, the year of the great solar eclipse. Also called THE ENGLISH ECLIPSE. The chestnut was only 14.2 hands but was never beaten in 18 races. Races then were 2 to 12 miles long, and horses did not race until they were at least 5 years old. He sired 300 winners, and 90 percent of top modern Thoroughbreds are descended from him, including the AMERICAN ECLIPSE.

Edward VII, King of England—see MINORU.

395. EEYORE—Winnie-the-Pooh's donkey friend that likes to eat thistles in A.A. Milne's book *Winnie-the-Pooh.*

396. EGYPT—One of Union General Ulysses S. Grant's Civil War chargers, a present from the people of Illinois.

EL BARAT—see AL BORAK.

El Cid Campeador—see BABIECA.

397. EL CORDOBES—A bay Andalusian stallion featured in photographer Robert Vavra's 1989 book *Vavra's Horses* as one of the ten most beautiful equines in the world.

The Electric Horseman, movie—see RISING STAR.

Eliot, George, author—see WILDFIRE (1280).

Elizabeth I, Queen of England—see AUREOLE, DEVON LOCH, MANICOU.

Elizabeth II, Queen of England—see ABOVE SUSPICION, ALEXANDER, BELLBOY, BETSY (116), BURMESE, BUSSACO, CENTENNIAL, COSSACK, DOUTELLE, HIGH VELDT, IMPERIAL, PRIDE, SULTAN, WINSTON.

Elizabeth, Queen Mother—see DEVON LOCH, HIGHCLERE MANICOU

El-Khamsa—see DAHMA, HADBA, HAMDANIEH, SAQLAWIEH, UBAYYAH.

Elliot, Gordon ("Wild Bill")—see STORMY (1133).

398. EL MORZILLO—The black stallion belonging to the Spanish explorer Hernando Cortes in the early 1500s while he was conquering Mexico. Cortes left the stallion with friendly Indians near present-day Guatemala after the horse was lamed by a hoof puncture. The Mayans worshiped the horse as the god Tziminchac, or Tziunchan (god of thunder and lightning), and fed him chicken, coconuts, pomegranates, papayas, figs, and bananas but the horse died of malnutrition. They erected a statue of the horse sitting on its haunches that was later destroyed by missionaries. MORZILLO means "black with a reddish luster."

el Sidi—see BABIECA.

399. ELWOOD—The 1904 Kentucky Derby winner, a bay colt.

400. EMPEROR—The white circus horse in William Makepeace Thackeray's *Ravenswing*. Also called HEMPEROR.

401. EMPRESS—A chestnut mare that won the Grand National Steeplechase in 1880.

402. ENBARR—Sea god Manannan's fleet horse in Celtic mythology. Name means "splendid mane."

ENGLISH ECLIPSE—see ECLIPSE (ENGLISH).

403. ENIK—One of the sacred horses of the sun, along with MENIK, BENIK, and SENIK, in Persian mythology.

Eos—see LAMPUS (660).

404. EOUS—One of sungod Apollo's wild white horses that pulled the fire chariot of the sun across the sky in classical mythology. Apollo's half-human son, Phaeton, tried to drive the chariot across the sky and failed.

405. EQUIPOISE—A great racehorse, also known as THE CHOCOLATE SOLDIER, that for many years held the record for the fastest mile in the history of American racing. He had DOMINO blood in him.

Equus, play—see NUGGET.

406. EROS—One of Messala's Arabian chariot horses in Lew Wallace's book, *Ben-Hur*.

407. ERYTHREOS—One of the horses belonging to Helios, the sun god in classical mythology.

408. ETHAN ALLEN—Descendant of JUSTIN MORGAN, son of BLACK HAWK, and one of the well-known stallions of that Morgan line. He won the Trotting Championship of the World in 1853. When he raced in 1867 against DEXTER, he trotted with a

running mate: a Thoroughbred was hitched to the sulky with shorter traces behind ETHAN ALLEN and galloped, leaving ETHAN ALLEN trotting free of the weight of the vehicle, and ETHAN ALLEN won that race.

Eutychus—see INCITATUS.

Evans, Dale—see BUTTERMILK (213), PAL (868).

Evans, Donald P., author—see RAMBLING WILLIE.

409. EXCELADDINN—A chestnut Arabian stallion featured in photographer Robert Vavra's 1989 book, *Vavra's Horses* as one of the world's ten most beautiful equines.

410. EXCELSIOR—General Nelson Miles' war-horse in the Civil War.

411. EXTERMINATOR—The 1918 Kentucky Derby winner, a chestnut gelding. He won 50 of 100 starts. He was also called BONES, THE GALLOPING HATRACK, OLD BONES, and SLIM. He had a pony companion named PEANUTS and later another called PEANUTS II. He died in 1945.

"F-Troop," television show—see PECOS.

The Faerie Queene—see BRIGADORE, SPUMADOR.

Faggus, Tom—see WINNIE.

412. FAIR PLAY—An ill-tempered chestnut stallion, the sire of MAN O'WAR. He was a runty runner that sulked, and his sire was HASTINGS.

413. FALABELLA—The smallest breed of horses, bred by Julio Falabella. He crossed small English Thorough-

breds with Shetland ponies. The Falabellas stand about 7 hands high.

414. FALADA—The talking horse belonging to the princess bride in the Grimms' fairytale, "Falada and the Goose-girl." The horse would speak only to the true bride, even after it is beheaded, and so saves the princess who had been forced to work as a goosegirl.

415. FALCON—Buster Crabbe's white horse in western movies.

416. FALKE—Dietrich von Bern's winged horse in German legend. Name means "falcon."

417. FANCY—A dark bay cob gelding, 13.3 hands, one of five horses that Velvet Brown inherited from Mr. Cellini in Enid Bagnold's book, *National Velvet*.

FANCY—see OLD SORREL.

418. FANNIE— One of Confederate General Joseph Johnston's Civil War horses, a bay Thoroughbred mare that was never wounded and retired to a farm after the war.

Faraway Farms—see MAN O'WAR.

Farley, Walter, author—see THE BLACK STALLION, CASS OLE, FLAME, NAPOLEON.

Farnum, Dustin—see PURGATORY.

419. FASHION—An 8-year-old chestnut mare that match-raced PEYTONA in 1845. PEYTONA won, and Currier and Ives made a print of the race.

420. FATHOM—The horse ridden by Diane Crump in 1970 as the first female jockey to race in the Kentucky Derby. She and FATHOM finished fifteenth.

421. FATIMA—Martha Washington's horse when she was a girl. She once rode the horse up the staircase of her house.

Faulkner, William, author—see LIGHTNING (679).

422. FAULTLESS—The actual winner of the 1947 Preakness, although JET PILOT had been incorrectly announced as the winner by Clem McCarthy.

423. FAUVEL—The noble steed ridden by King Richard I (the Lion-Hearted) during the Crusades. The light sorrel Arabian was killed at the Battle of Jaffa. Also spelled FLAVELLE.

424. FAVORY—One of the foundation sires of the well-known Lippizan horses of the Spanish Riding School.

Federal Bureau of Investigation—see ZACHREGARD.

Ferber, Edna, author—see MY MISTAKE.

425. FERDINAND—The 1986 Kentucky Derby winner, a chestnut colt with a white star. He was ridden by 54-year-old Bill Shoemaker in his fourth Derby win, and had a 73-year-old trainer. FERDINAND, a long shot, was last at the half-mile mark but won the race by 2 ½ lengths.

Fergus, Dirty Sally—see WORTHLESS.

Ferrari—see THE PRANCING HORSE.

426. FIDELITY—Theodore Roosevelt's daughter, Ethel's pet horse.

The Fighting 69th, movie—see GERMAINE.

The Fighting Stallion, movie—see REX (976).

FIGURE—see JUSTIN MORGAN.

Fillmore, President Millard—see LEXINGTON (676).

427. FINALITY—Pat Smythe's first show jumper in the late 1940s.

428. FIRE-EATER—One of Confederate General Albert Johnston's Civil war chargers, a bay Thoroughbred wounded four times in the war.

429. FIREFLY—General Isaac Sherwood's war-horse in the Civil War, a black mare that died in the Battle of Franklin.

430. FIREFLY—A horse owned and ridden by Rudolph Valentino in the movie *The Son of the Sheik*.

431. FIRPON—The tallest horse on record, a Percheron-Shire cross owned by Julio Falabella that stood 21.1 hands high and died in 1972 at the age of 13. Falabella also owned miniature horses.

432. FIVE MINUTES TO MIDNIGHT—A champion rodeo bucking horse whose name was a spin-off of the former champion bucker MIDNIGHT.

433. FLAG OF LEYTE GULF—The racehorse that jockey Ron Turcotte rode on July 13, 1978, in his 20,310th race. The horse was bumped and went down. Ron was paralyzed from the waist down in the accident and is now confined to a wheelchair. Ron was SECRETAR-IAT's jockey in the 1973 Triple Crown wins.

434. FLAME—The chestnut stallion in the Walter Farley book, *The Island Stallion*.

FLAME—see GHOST.

435. FLAMING TRON KU—A dapple-gray Arabian stallion racehorse featured in photographer Robert Vavra's

1989 book, *Vavra's Horses,* as one of the world's ten most beautiful equines.

436. FLANAGAN—The chestnut gelding that Pat Smythe rode in the 1956 Olympics as part of the British Equestrian Team. Pat was the first woman to compete in Olympic equestrian events.

437. FLANAKINS—A horse that died in a racing accident. His jockey, Ralph Newes, was first thought to have also been killed in the accident, but he lived.

Flap, movie—see H BOMB.

438. FLASH—A white horse ridden by Gary Cooper in the 1927 movies *Arizona Bound* and *The Last Outlaw.*

439. FLASH—One of Eddie Dean's horses in western movies.

FLAVELLE—see FAUVEL.

440. FLEDGE—The talking horse in C.S. Lewis's *The Magician's Nephew,* sixth in the series, *The Chronicles of Narnia.*

THE FLEET—see COUNT FLEET.

441. FLEET DRIVER—Johnny Longden's mount in 1952 when he won his 4,000th race, the first jockey to do so.

442. FLICKA—The filly in Mary O'Hara's books, *My Friend Flicka* and *Thunderhead.* Name means "young girl" in Norwegian. Also the name of the horse in the television show, "My Friend Flicka," 1956–1964 that was played by an Arabian mare named WAHAMA. In the 1943 movie, an American Saddlebred Horse played FLICKA. FLICKA was Ken McLaughlin's filly in the story and was very difficult to tame.

443. FLORA TEMPLE—The first harness trotter to do the mile in less than 2:20, she was a small, bobtail bay mare who lived in the 1850's and was the bobtail nag of the song, "Camptown Races." She lowered her own world record five times in her career.

444. FLORIAN—The Lippizan stallion in Felix Salten's book, *Florian*. He was played by a white Lippizan stallion named PLUTO in the movie *Florian*.

445. FLY—Laura Ingalls Wilder's husband Manly's saddle horse.

446. FLYING EBONY—The 1925 Kentucky Derby winner, a black colt.

FLYING RED HORSE—see PEGASUS (888).

THE FLYING TAIL—see WHIRLAWAY.

447. FOFO—The horse in Luigi Pirandello's story, "Black Horses."

Fonda, Jane—see RISING STAR.

448. FONSO—The 1880 Kentucky Derby winner, a chestnut colt.

449. FOOLISH PLEASURE—The 1975 Kentucky Derby winner, a bay colt. He was in a match race in 1975 against the 3-year-old filly RUFFIAN in which RUFFIAN broke her ankle and was put down.

Forbes, Bryan, author—see ARIZONA PIE.

450. FOREGO—One of the richest racehorses ever, winning $1,923,957.

451. FORIO—A horse with a broken leg that was shot in the 1964 movie, *Marnie*.

Forrest, Nathan Bedford—see KING PHILIP.

FORWARD PASS—see DANCER'S IMAGE.

452. FOX—One of Union General Ulysses S. Grant's horses during the Civil War, a powerful roan.

453. FOX—A great dressage horse ridden by Tonny Jensen.

THE FOX—see GALLANT FOX.

THE FOX OF BELAIR—see GALLANT FOX.

454. FOXHUNTER—A 16.3-hand, bay Thoroughbred-Clydesdale cross, a show-jumping horse ridden and trained by Colonel Harry M. Llewellyn in the late 1940s and early 1950s. They were part of the British Olympic team in 1952 and retired in 1956 after many international wins. FOXHUNTER was foaled in 1940 and died in 1959.

455. FRANCIS—The talking-mule star of television and movies. His voice was provided by Chill Wills.

Francis, Dick, jockey and author—see DEVON LOCH.

456. FRECKLES—The horse belonging to Dusty, the trail scout in the 1973 television show, "Dusty's Trail."

457. FRED—A North Carolina horse in the early 1900s that pulled a hose wagon to fires. He died in 1925, and his head is on display in the Firemen's Museum in New Bern, North Carolina.

Frederick the Great, King of Prussia—see CONDE.

458. FRESH YANKEE—A trotter mare in the 1960s and 1970s.

Frey—see BLODIGHOFI, FREYFAXI.

Frey, Johnny—see SYLPH.

Freya—see SVADILFARI.

459. FREYFAX—Brand's white-maned war-horse in Nordic mythology.

460. FREYFAXI—One of Frey's horses in Nordic mythology.

The Friendly Persuasion, book and movie—see LADY, RED ROVER.

461. FRIGATE—The mare that won the Grand National Steeplechase in 1889.

Frigga—see HOFVARPNIR.

Fritsch, Captain Frederick Otto—see CAESAR (222), JIM (598).

462. FRITZ—The pinto cow horse that worked with William S. Hart in early western movies and lived to the age of 31. Hart and FRITZ used no stunt doubles for their 1920s movies, which included *Pinto Ben* and *The Narrow Trail.* Hart's horse CACTUS KATE and pack mule LISABETH were devoted to the gelding FRITZ.

463. FROU FROU—An English Thoroughbred mare in Leo Tolstoy's book, *Anna Karenina.*

464. FRU-FRU—An Arabian horse ridden by Italian dictator Benito Mussolini in the early 1920s.

465. FUBUKI—The snow-white Albino stallion sent to Japan in 1938 at Emperor Hirohito's request to be his mount. Name means "snow," and he was once a cow horse named SILVER TIP.

Funston, Frederick—see WILLIE GROW.

466. FURY—The famous black American Saddlebred stallion, star of television and movies, whose name originally was HIGHLAND DALE. He played Joey Newton's horse in the television show "Fury," 1955–1956; and he starred in the movies, *Black Beauty,* 1946; *Gypsy Colt,* 1955; *Giant,* 1956; and *Wild Is the Wind,* 1958. He was owned and trained by Ralph McCutcheon after he was purchased in Colorado at the age of 1½.

467. FURY—Indian Straight Arrow's golden palomino horse on the radio show, "Straight Arrow," in the late 1940s.

"Fury," television show—see FURY (466), LUCKY, POKEY (921).

468. FURY JR.—A movie horse owned and trained by Ralph McCutcheon. FURY JR. was the son of McCutcheon's original FURY.

469. FYVIE—A Highland pony used by Queen Victoria when she was middle-aged.

470. GABILAN—The red pony in John Steinbeck's book, *The Red Pony.* The pony is owned by Jody and dies in the book. Name means "the hawk."

Gable, Clark—see BABA, BEAUTY (102), BOOTS.

Gabriel—see HAIZUM.

471. GAI PARADA—A light gray Arabian stallion featured in photographer Robert Vavra's 1989 book, *Vavra's Horses,* as one of the world's ten most beautiful equines.

472. GAIGNUN—Pagan Marsilon's war-horse in the epic poem, *The Song of Roland.* Name means "watchdog."

473. GAINES DENMARK—A black stallion that both was a great show horse and was ridden for two years in the

Civil War. The 15.2-hand stallion with two white socks was foaled in 1851 and died in 1864. He was a foundation sire for the American Saddle Horse breed, and was also called BLACK DENMARK.

474. GALATHE—Hector's horse in William Shakespeare's play, *Troilus and Cressida.*

475. GALLAHADION—The 1940 Kentucky Derby winner, a bay colt.

476. GALLANT FOX—The 1930 Triple Crown winner, a bay colt, also called THE FOX and THE FOX OF BELAIR. The white-blazed horse was lazy as a 2-year-old but overcame that. He went on to sire the 1935 Triple Crown winner OMAHA. GALLANT FOX died at age 27 in 1954.

477. GALLANT MAN—Ridden by Bill Shoemaker in the 1957 Kentucky Derby, he lost to IRON LIEGE by a nose because Shoemaker misjudged the finish line and stood up in the stirrups before the race was over.

GALLOPING HATRACK—see EXTERMINATOR.

478. GALLORETTE—A well-known chestnut racehorse, a mare.

Galsworthy, John, author—see CALLIOPE, HANGMAN, PARROT, THE SHIRKER.

479. GAMAL—A bay gelding that performed a diving act in Atlantic City, New Jersey, in the 1970s. He dove off a 40-foot tower with a rider on his back into a 12-foot-deep tank of water.

Gandalf—see SHADOWFAX.

Ganelon—see TACHEBRUN.

Garfield, Molly—see KIT.

480. GARGANTUA'S MARE—A horse as big as six elephants in Francois Rabelais's *Gargantua and Pantagruel.*

Garibaldi, Giuseppe—see MARSALA.

Garnett, Richard—see RED EYE.

481. GATO—An Argentine Criollo pony ridden, along with MANCHA, by Aime F. Tschiffely from Buenos Aires, Argentina, to Washington, D.C., a 2 ½-year (1925–1927) trip of nearly 10,000 miles. The name means "cat." GATO, a coffee-colored buckskin with faint black stripes, was 15 and wild at the beginning of the trip, which Tschiffely undertook in order to show the world what a hardy breed the Criollos were. GATO died in 1944, and his body is on exhibit at the Colonial Museum in Lujan near Buenos Aires.

482. GATO DEL SOL—The 1982 Kentucky Derby winner, a gray colt named after a sun-loving cat. He was last at the half-mile marker but won the race by 2 ½ lengths.

Gawain, Sir—see GRINGALET.

Geiger, Emily—see UNKNOWN HORSE (1230).

"The Gene Autry Show," television show—see CHAMPION.

483. GENERAL—A gray horse ridden by Confederate General Jeb Stuart in the Battle of Yellow Tavern in 1864 where Stuart was mortally wounded.

484. THE GENERAL—President John Tyler's favorite horse.

Genter, Frances—see UNBRIDLED.

485. GENUINE RISK—The 1980 Kentucky Derby winner, a chestnut filly with a white blaze. Winning by a length, she was the second filly ever to win the Kentucky Derby and the first to win in 65 years.

486. GEORGE—A chestnut pony gelding, 12.2 hands, one of five horses that Velvet Brown inherited from Mr. Cellini in Enid Bagnold's book, *National Velvet*.

George V, King of England—see JOCK.

487. GEORGE SMITH—The 1916 Kentucky Derby winner, a black colt.

Gerier—see PASSECERF.

Gerin—see SOREL.

488. GERMAINE—A mule that won the Animal Actor Of the Year award in 1940 after starring in the movie, *The Fighting 69th*.

Germinal—see BATAILLE.

489. GERONIMO—Horse ridden by 6-year-old Templeton Abernathy for 2,500 miles to meet Colonel Teddy Roosevelt in 1910. The trip, from Oklahoma to New York, took Templeton, his 10-year-old brother Louis, and Louis's horse SAM six weeks.

490. GERTIE—The horse in Margarite Glendinning's book, *Gertie the Horse*.

491. GERTRUDE—A mare that was bred with BLACK ALLAN. Their get was ROAN ALLEN, one of the first Tennessee Walking Horses.

492. GHOST—A great movie horse, the only horse able to fall on cue. His stage name was FLAME, and he starred in some of the Zane Grey western movies.

Giant, book and movie—see BEAUTY (102), FURY (466), MY MISTAKE.

493. GIBRALTAR—One of Philip Astley's performing horses in the late 18th century. Astley's shows were the beginning of the modern circus. GIBRALTAR died at age 42.

Gibson, Hoot—see GOLDIE, MUTT, STARLIGHT (1122), WHITEY (1276).

Gillespie, Lieutenant Archibald—see UNKNOWN HORSES (1233).

Gilmour, H.B., author—see RISING STAR.

GIMME A C—see NEWCOMER.

494. GINGER—One of BLACK BEAUTY's harness mates, a sensitive and temperamental chestnut mare, in Anna Sewell's book, *Black Beauty.*

Gipson, Fred, author—see JUMPER.

495. GITANA—The horse in Francis Kalnay's book, *Chacaro, Wild Pony of the Pampas.* Name means "gypsy."

496. GJATSK—Soviet chestnut Thoroughbred colt that ran in the Washington, D.C., International in 1988, the first time in 21 years that the Soviets had an entry in the race. GJATSK finished next to last.

497. GLADSTONE—The horse that drew the Cherrelyn car in Englewood, Colorado, around 1904. GLAD-STONE would draw the car to the top of the hill, then jump onto the platform on his own for the ride back down the hill.

Gleason, Jackie—see TOSSY.

498. GLENCOE—One of Confederate General John Hunt Morgan's Thoroughbred war-horses in the Civil War.

Glendinning, Margarite, author—see GERTIE.

499. GLORY—The fictional winner of the Kentucky Derby in the 1956 movie, *Glory*.

Gna—see HOFVARPNIR.

500. GO FOR WAND—The 3-year-old filly that had almost won the televised 1990 Breeder's Cup Distaff race when she broke her leg and fell. She was humanely destroyed at the racetrack.

501. GO GET LOST—A 4-year-old trotter that liked to eat Hostess chocolate cupcakes. When he won a race in 1988, he was presented with a silver trophy filled with them.

The Godfather, movie—see KHARTOUM.

Godfrey, Arthur—see ALYFAR.

502. THE GODOLPHIN BARB—One of the three Arabian stallions imported into England to found the English Thoroughbred line. Foaled in 1724, imported by King Charles II from Paris, he was grandsire of MATCHEM. It is said that he was discovered pulling a water cart in Paris, and was sold to Lord Godolphin in 1730 as a teaser stallion. He was also called THE GODOLPHIN ARABIAN. His story was fictionalized in Marguerite Henry's book *King of the Wind.* The other two horses were THE BYERLY TURK and THE DARLEY ARABIAN.

503. GOLD DOUBLOON—A palomino Paso Fino stallion featured in photographer Robert Vavra's 1989 book, *Vavra's Horses,* as one of the world's ten most beautiful equines.

504. GOLDIE—Hoot Gibson's golden palomino horse in western movies.

505. GOLDSMITH MAID—A successful trotter mare in the 1860s and 1870s.

506. GOLIATH—The black Friesian horse that Captain Navarre rides in the 1985 fantasy movie, *Ladyhawke,* based on European legend.

   Gone with the Wind, movie—see MARSE ROBERT.

507. GOOD TIME—A great pacer in the 1940s and 1950s, the winning pacer of his time.

508. GOODWILL—Princess Anne's British Equestrian Team mount for the 1976 Olympic Three-Day Event.

   The Goosegirl—see FALADA.

   Gordon, John—see MARYE.

509. GOVERNATORE—The favorite horse of King Henry VIII of England.

510. GRACE DARLING—A mare ridden by Robert E. Lee in the Mexican War.

   Gradasso—see ALFANA.

   Graham, Helen Holland, author—see CHICKO.

   Grahame, Kenneth, author—see CYRIL.

511. GRANAT—A great dressage horse ridden by Christine Stuckelberger.

   Grandoigne—see MARMOIRE.

512. GRANI—The marvelously swift gray horse belonging to Siegfried, the medieval knight and legendary hero of

the German epic, *The Nibelungenlied* and of Wagner's opera, *Siegfried*. After Siegfried's death, GRANI was ridden onto the funeral pyre by Siegfried's true love Brunhilde. His name is also spelled GRANE, and it means "gray." Sigurd is GRANI's owner in Norse legend.

Grant, Ulysses S.—see CHARLIE (256), CINCINNATI, EGYPT, FOX (452), ISMAEL, JACK (577), JEFF DAVIS (593), KANGAROO, LEGAL TENDER, LEOPARD, LINDEN TREE.

513. GRAY GHOST—Chief Sitting Bull's trained horse in William F. ("Buffalo Bill") Cody's Wild West shows.

THE GRAY GHOST—see NATIVE DANCER.

514. THE GRAY OF MACHA—Celtic warrior Cuchulainn's magic chariot horse, in Irish legend. A mare foaled at the same time that Cuchulainn, the Irish Achilles, was born, and the two foals, THE GRAY OF MACHA and THE BLACK OF SAINGLEND, were given to him.

515. THE GREAT HORSE—The horse in a painting by Albrecht Durer. The horse is from the 16th century, and the Shire Horse is said to have descended from him.

GREENBRIER—see TRAVELLER (1203).

516. GREGALACH—The horse that won the 1929 Grand National Steeplechase. There were 66 starters, which was a record number, and GREGALACH won at 100 to 1 odds.

517. GREYHOUND—A 16.2-hand gray gelding Standardbred harness horse, foaled in 1932. His stride measured 23 feet. He set 25 world records in the 1930s, then did exhibitions because no one wanted to race against him. He retired in 1940 and died at the age of 33 in 1965.

518. GREYHOUND—A gray racehorse owned by Andrew Jackson that was in a match race against TRUXTON.

519. GRINGALET—Gawain's steed from the poem *Sir Gawain and the Green Knight*. Also spelled GRINGOLET.

520. GRIZZLE—An old gray mare seen in a series of artistic plates titled, *The Tour of Doctor Syntax in Search of the Picturesque*, by William Combe and Thomas Rowlandson.

521. GUALIANKO—A white Arabian owned by President Ronald Reagan.

Guinan, Texas—see SNOWFLAKE (1099).

522. GULLFAXI—The horse belonging to the giant Hrimgrim in Norse mythology.

Gulliver's Travels, book—see HOUYHNHNMS.

Gumby—see POKEY (922).

523. GUNPOWDER—The old, broken-down, and partially blind horse Ichabod Crane rides home in Washington Irving's *Legend of Sleepy Hollow*.

"Gunsmoke," television show—see CUCO BRITCHES, MARSHAL, RUTH.

Gurney, Hilda—see KEEN.

Gustavus Adolphus, King of Sweden—see STREIFF.

Guyon, Sir—see BRIGADORE.

Gypsy Colt, movie—see FURY (466).

524. H BOMB—Star of the 1973 movie, *Flap*, a horse that drank whiskey. He was played by a horse named OLD FOOLER.

525. HADBA—One of the five gallant Arabian mares that passed the endurance test in Mecca in the 7th century and founded the most notable families of Arabian horses. All five are referred to as El-Khamsa ("the Five"), or Al Khamseh. HADBA was red, and her name means "lady with long eyelashes."

Haggen, Festus—see RUTH.

526. HAIZUM—Gabriel's horse in Islamic stories.

Hale, Monte—see PARDNER (875).

527. HALF BAR—The chestnut sorrel American Quarter Horse sired by THREE BARS.

528. HALLA—Hans Winkler's 17-hand half-bred show jumping mare. They competed in the 1956 and 1960 Olympics.

529. HALMA—The 1895 Kentucky Derby winner, a black colt.

Hamblen, Stuart—see TOMBOY.

530. HAMBLETONIAN—Foaled in 1849 in New York, a great-grandson of MESSENGER, and a pillar of the Standardbred line. He was a dark bay foal of ABDALLAH, an unpopular Thoroughbred sire, and a crippled mare. The 15.2-hand bay, with a white star and two white socks, was bought by William Rysdyk for $125. He was named after a well-known trotter of earlier times. Ninety-nine percent of trotters and pacers in America trace to HAMBLETONIAN, including DICTATOR. The stud book lists him as HAMBLETONIAN 10, and he is also known as RYSDYK'S HAMBLETONIAN. HAMBLETONIAN himself never raced but stood at stud for 24 years, siring great trotters and pacers. He died in 1876 at the age of 27.

531. HAMDANIEH—One of the five gallant Arabian mares that passed the endurance test in Mecca in the 7th century and founded the most notable families of Arabian horses. All five are referred to as El-Khamsa ("the Five"), or Al Khamseh. HAMDANIEH was a bay, and her name means "after the family name."

Hammond, Captain Charles—see JEFF (591), PINK.

Hampton, General Wade—see BEAUREGARD, BUTLER.

Handley, Dick—see CORNCRACKER.

532. HANGMAN—The 5-year-old racehorse in John Galsworthy's book, *Caravan: The Assembled Tales of John Galsworthy*. HANGMAN raced in the short story "Had a Horse."

533. HANNIBAL—Ben Calhoun's horse in the television show "The Iron Horse," 1966–1968. Also Dale Robertson's black Quarter Horse in the movie *The Iron Horse*.

534. HANOVER—A Thoroughbred stallion foaled in 1884 and sired by HINDOO.

Harbut, Will—see MAN O'WAR.

The Hard Servant—see THE MEAN MARE.

HARO—see HERO.

The Harpy Podarge—see BALIUS, XANTHUS (1296).

535. HARRY—One of Union General George A. Custer's war-horses during the Civil War. The horse was named after Custer's nephew.

Hart, Sam—see BETSY (117), SALOME.

Hart, William S.—see CACTUS KATE, FRITZ, LISA-BETH.

Hartack, Bill—see DECIDEDLY, IRON LIEGE, MA-JESTIC PRINCE, NORTHERN DANCER, VENE-TIAN WAY.

Haskell, Lieutenant Frank—see BILLY (127), DICK (346).

Haslam, Robert, "Pony Bob"—see UNKNOWN HORSES (1234).

536. HASTINGS—The sire of FAIR PLAY and the grand-sire of MAN O'WAR. He tried to bite other horses on the racetrack.

Hatch, Eric, author—see ASPERCEL.

537. HATSUSHIMO—Japanese Emperor Hirohito's favor-ite Albino horse, foaled in 1927. Name means "white frost."

"Have Gun, Will Travel," television show—see RAF-TER.

Hawthorne, Nathaniel, author—see PEGASUS (886).

Hayes, Gabby—see BLOOSOM, CALICO.

538. HEARTLIGHT NO. ONE—A 3-year-old racehorse, a filly, owned by Burt Bacharach and Carol Bayer, and named after the song written by them and Neil Diamond.

539. HEATHCLIFFE—The puppet Snarkey Parker's horse in the 1950 television show, "Life with Snarkey Parker."

540. HEATHERBLOOM—A performing horse that once jumped 8 feet 3 inches. Barnum and Bailey Circus offered $25,000 for him.

Hector—see AETHON (13), GALATHE, LAMPUS (659), PODARGUS, XANTHUS (1297).

Helios—see AETHON (12), AMETHEA, BRONTE, ERYTHREOS, LAMPOS, PHLEGON, PYROIS.

HEMPEROR—see EMPEROR.

Hendricks, Byron—see LEGENDAIRE.

Henry IV, Pt. I, play—see CUT.

Henry V, movie—see BLAUNCHKYNG.

Henry VIII, King of England—see GOVERNATORE.

Henry, Marguerite, author—see BLACK COMET, BRIGHTY, EBENEZER (389), JUSTIN MORGAN, MISTY (784), PHANTOM (897), PIED PIPER, SAN DOMINGO, SEA STAR, SHAM, STORMY (1134).

Hercules—see ARION, THE MARES OF DI-OMEDES.

541. HERO—One of the Phantom's horses in the comic strip "The Phantom."

542. HERO—Confederate Lieutenant General James Long-street's favorite intelligent bay charger in the Civil War. His groom had an accent and pronounced the name HARO.

543. HEROD—Horse foaled in 1758 whose great-great-grandsire was THE BYERLY TURK. HEROD was a foundation sire of the Thoroughbred horse.

Herr, E.D.—see BLACK ALLAN.

Heston, Charlton—see ALDEBARAN, ANTARES, ATAIR, DOMINO (362), RIGEL.

544. HI HAT—Harpo Marx's racehorse in the 1937 movie, *A Day at the Races*.

Hickok, James Butler ("Wild Bill")—see BLACK NELL, BUCKSHOT.

545. HIDALGO—The only horse other than an Arabian to have won, in 1899, the 3,000-mile endurance race in Arabia, a pinto stallion owned by Frank T. Hopkins.

546. HIGH JINKS—A pony ridden by Princess Anne as a child.

547. HIGH SKY—One of Confederate General Jeb Stuart's horses in the Civil War.

548. HIGH VELDT—A horse owned by Queen Elizabeth II of England that won the 1956 2000 Guineas Trial Stakes and was the second of three consecutive winners of that race for her.

549. HIGHCLERE—A racehorse filly, owned by the Queen Mother that won the 1000 Guineas and the French Oaks races.

HIGHLAND DALE—see FURY (466).

550. HILL GAIL—The 1952 Kentucky Derby winner, a dark bay colt. His jockey was Eddie Arcaro, who has ridden five Kentucky Derby winners.

551. HILL PRINCE—A well-known bay racehorse.

552. HIMYAR—The sire of DOMINO, a racehorse.

553. HINDOO—The 1881 Kentucky Derby winner, a bay colt.

Hinton, S.E., author—see NEGRITO.

554. HIPPOCAMPUS—The sea horse in classical mythology that had the upper body of a horse and the lower body of a fish. He drew Poseidon's chariot over the sea.

Hirohito, Emperor of Japan—see FUBUKI, HATSU-SHIMO.

555. HIRONDELLE—The mare that Madame Chatelet rode while accompanying French writer Voltaire on his hunts. Name means "swallow."

556. HIS EMINENCE—The 1901 Kentucky Derby winner, a bay colt.

Hitchcock, Thomas—see OLD SHORTY.

557. HOFVARPNIR—The horse owned by Frigga, the Norse goddess of love and springtime. Name refers to the personification of the refreshing breeze that tosses his hooves. Ridden by the goddess Gna on errands for Frigga.

558. HOIST THE FLAG—A Thoroughbred racehorse that was the favorite for the 1971 Kentucky Derby, but broke a leg during a workout before the race.

Holt, Tim—see DUKE (382), LIGHTNING (680).

Homer, poet—see AETHON (13), ARION, BALIUS, LAMPUS (659), PODARGUS, THE TROJAN HORSE (1209), XANTHUS (1297).

559. HONEY—One of the horses that pulled the Overland Stage in the 1939 movie, *Stagecoach,* starring John Wayne. Andy Devine drove the stage and shouted encouragement to the horses. There were three hitches of six horses each used on the stagecoach route.

Hooker, General Joseph—see LOOKOUT (698).

560. HOOP JR.—The 1945 Kentucky Derby winner, a bay colt. His jockey was Eddie Arcaro, who has ridden five Kentucky Derby winners.

Hoover, President Herbert—see BLACK JACK.

Hopalong Cassidy—see BANJO, PEPPER, TOPPER.

Hopkins, Frank T.—see HIDALGO.

561. HORACE HORSECOLLAR—A horse in early Mickey Mouse cartoons.

The Horse and His Boy, book—see BREE, HWIN.

Horse in Danger, book—see INKY.

The Horse in the Gray Flannel Suit, movie—see ASPER-CEL.

A Horse's Tale, story—see SOLDIER BOY.

Houston, Sam —see BRUIN, JACK (580), OLD PETE.

562. HOUYHNHNMS—The race of horses that represented nobility, virtue, and reason in Jonathan Swift's book, *Gulliver's Travels*.

"How They Brought the Good News from Ghent to Aix", poem—see ROLAND.

Hoxie, Al—see PARDNER (874).

Hoxie, Jack—see SCOUT (1041), WHITE FURY.

563. HRIMFAXI—In Norse mythology this black horse was driven across the sky by the goddess of the night Nott.

Hrimgrim—see GULLFAXI.

564. HUASO—The horse that set the equestrian high-jump record of 8 feet, 1 ¼ inches in 1949, ridden by Captain Larraguibel Morales in Chile.

565. HUD—Paul Newman's horse's real name in the 1969 movie, *Butch Cassidy and the Sundance Kid.*

566. HWIN—A talking mare in C.S. Lewis's book, *The Horse and His Boy,* the fifth in the series, *The Chronicles of Narnia.*

567. HYPERION—A small English Thoroughbred horse with four white socks that was bred and owned by Lord Derby. Foaled in 1930, he won the English Derby in 1933 and also the St. Leger. He was put down in 1960 due to paralysis in his legs.

568. IDLE DICE—One of Rodney Jenkins' famous show jumpers, a gelding.

Iliad—see AETHON (13), ARION, BALIUS, LAMPUS (659), PODARGUS, THE TROJAN HORSE (1209), XANTHUS (1297).

569. IMPERIAL—A horse ridden by Queen Elizabeth II in ceremonial parades in the 1970s.

IMPORTED MESSENGER—see MESSENGER.

570. INCITATUS—A stallion almost named consul of the empire by the mad Roman Emperor Gaius Caesar (known as Caligula, i.e., "Little Boots") around A.D. 40. The horse was originally Eutychus' chariot racing horse and was named PORCELLUS ("Little Pig") until Caligula renamed him and took him over. INCITATUS had a marble manger, an ivory stall, a bucket of gold, a jeweled collar, and a number of slaves who served him. Caligula thought that the horse was the only living thing he could trust, and he made him a citizen, a senator, and a priest, but was assasinated by his own guard before he

could make the horse a consul. INCITATUS means "swift speeding," "go ahead," or "flyer" in Latin.

571. INDIAN WOMAN—Actor David Carradine's Appaloosa mare.

572. INKY—The horse in Glenn Balch's book, *Horse in Danger.*

Innocents Abroad, book—see JERICHO.

International Velvet, book and movie—see ARIZONA PIE.

The Iron Duke—see COPENHAGEN.

THE IRON HORSE—see DISPLAY.

The Iron Horse, television show and movie—see HANNIBAL.

573. IRON LIEGE—The 1957 Kentucky Derby winner, a bay colt. His jockey was Bill Hartack, who has ridden five Kentucky Derby winners. GALLANT MAN came in second.

574. IROQUOIS—The first American-bred horse to win the English Derby, in 1881, and the only one to do so up to 1946. IROQUOIS was born in 1878 and died in 1899.

Irving, Washington, author—see GUNPOWDER, DAREDEVIL.

575. ISHAM—William F. ("Buffalo Bill") Cody's favorite show horse, a snow white horse that he had for over 20 years. The horse was a gift from painter Rosa Bonheur, who painted their picture. When the Wild West Show was closed due to bankruptcy, a friend purchased ISHAM at the auction to give back to Cody. ISHAM

was not the white horse at Cody's funeral in 1917—that was a livery stable horse.

Ishmael—see KUHAYLAH.

The Island Stallion, book—see FLAME (434).

576. ISMAEL—An Arabian stallion belonging to General Ulysses S. Grant.

It Ain't Hay, movie—see TEABISCUIT.

577. JACK—A cream-colored stallion ridden by Union General Ulysses S. Grant early in the Civil War. His color was too conspicuous on the battlefield so he was auctioned off at a benefit for the wounded.

578. JACK—A horse owned by George Washington and sold to John Bill Rickett's circus at age 28.

579. JACK—The pony that Tom pushed to gallop and jump for too many miles in Hilaire Belloc's book, *New Cautionary Tales for Children.*

580. JACK—A tailless horse belonging to Sam Houston in the mid-1800s.

581. JACK RUCKER—Union Captain George A. Custer's bay horse in the Civil War. The horse was a fine racer, and Custer won many bets on him.

582. JACKSON—A horse owned by George Washington that was depicted in a famous equestrian portrait of Washington.

Jackson, Andrew—see GREYHOUND (518), TRUXTON.

Jackson, Thomas J. ("Stonewall")—see OLD SORREL.

583. JADAAN—Rudolph Valentino's gray Arabian stallion in the 1926 movie, *The Son of the Sheik.*

584. JAFFA—One of Napoleon Bonaparte's favorite white war-horses.

585. JAKE—One of the Budweiser Clydesdale geldings from the eight-horse hitch that toured the fourteen western states.

586. JALALI—A magic talking horse chosen by David of Sassoun in Armenian legend. Name is Arabic for "robber" or "outlaw."

James, Frank—see DAN.

James, Jesse—see CYROCK, KATIE, RED FOX.

James, Will, author —see CHARRO, COLONEL (276), RAGTIME, SMOKY.

587. JAMIN—A French trotter that liked to eat artichokes and that won the American International Trot in 1959. When he first came to America he was unhappy because his French artichokes had been confiscated. California artichokes had to be flown in for the horse so that he could train well and win.

Jane Eyre, book—see MESROUR.

588. JANUS—The first great foundation sire of the sprinting Quarter Horse, a small chestnut stallion that was imported to Virginia in the 1750s from England. He was a racer but not a true Thoroughbred, and he also influenced the American Saddle Horse breed.

589. JAY TRUMP—An American steeplechasing gelding that won the English Grand National in 1965 and the American Maryland Hunt Cup race in 1966, ridden by Tommy Smith, an amateur. Foaled on April 1, 1957,

this scarred, flat-track reject bay with a white star overcame injuries and a unique jumping style to win these races. He was the first American-bred, American-trained, and American-ridden horse to win the Grand National, and the first to win both the Grand National and the Maryland Hunt Cup. JAY TRUMP retired in 1966.

590. JEB STUART—One of Confederate Henry Douglas's war-horses in the Civil War that performed well in battle. He was stolen from Douglas later in the war.

591. JEFF—One of Union Captain Charles Hammond's war-horses in the Civil War that had been captured in Virginia. He survived the war and died in a pasture accident. His name is on a stone shaft in New York state commemorating the men of Company H and their horses.

592. JEFF—One of General John Pershing's horses, a Virginia hunter.

593. JEFF DAVIS—A black pony that was captured from Confederate President Jefferson Davis's brother's plantation during the Civil War. Union General Ulysses S. Grant gave the pony to his son to ride, but his son had to loan the pony to Grant when he was in need of a comfortable horse. The pony's gaits were smooth, and Grant liked him very much. Grant cared for him till he died long after the war. Also called LITTLE JEFF.

JEFF DAVIS—see TRAVELLER (1203).

Jefferson, Thomas—see EAGLE.

Jenkins, Lucky—see BANJO.

Jenkins, Pee Wee—see POKEY (921).

Jenkins, Rodney—see IDLE DICE, NUMBER ONE SPY.

594. JENNY CAMP—The 16.1-hand U.S. Army–bred horse that was part of the United States Three-Day Event Team in the 1936 Olympics in Berlin. Many horses fell at one jump in the cross-country phase, but not the German mounts. Some people thought that Hitler engineered a faulty jump and told only the German riders how to avoid it in order to ensure German winners. JENNY CAMP, ridden by Captain Earl F. Thompson, also fell but was able to finish the course and all of the other Three-Day events. Her teammates did not do so well (one broke a leg and had to be destroyed). JENNY CAMP outscored all the German horses individually, but her team was disqualified.

595. JENNY GEDDES —The old hunter mare about whom Robert Burns wrote the poem, "Epistle to Hugh Parker" in 1788.

Jensen, Tonny—see FOX (453).

596. JERICHO—The mare in Mark Twain's book, *Innocents Abroad* that had a short tail and fought flies with her heels.

597. JET PILOT—The 1947 Kentucky Derby winner, a chestnut colt that won wire to wire. He ran in the 1947 Preakness as well and was incorrectly named the winner by announcer Clem McCarthy. FAULTLESS was the real winner.

598. JIM—Union Captain Frederick Otto Fritsch's second war-horse in the Civil War.

599. JIM—A horse ridden by Robert E. Lee in the Mexican War.

600. JIM DANDY—Raced against 1930 Triple Crown winner GALLANT FOX in 1930 and won at 100 to 1 odds.

Joan of Arc—see UNKNOWN HORSES (1226).

601. JOCK—The favorite horse of King George V of England; Jock was a white cob.

Jody—see GABILAN.

602. JOE COTTON—The 1885 Kentucky Derby winner, a bay colt.

603. JOE HANCOCK—Quarter Horse stallion foaled in the mid-1920s. The dark brown stallion was part Percheron and influenced the American Quarter Horse breed. JOE HANCOCK was put down in 1943 due to founder.

604. JOHN HENRY—A bay Thoroughbred racehorse gelding that had been purchased for $25,000 and won $6.5 million in his long and arduous career. At age 9 he won over $2 million in one year. He retired at age 10 in 1986.

605. JOHN P. GRIER—Racehorse that match-raced against MAN O'WAR in 1920. He was neck and neck most of the way and even got a slight lead at one point, but MAN O'WAR won by 1 ½ lengths.

606. JOHN THE BAPTIST—A light brown horse with roan spots that was used in a carnival diving act around 1924. Sonora Carver rode the horse off a 40-foot tower into an 11-foot tank of water. He was the smoothest diver of all the horses she rode.

Johnny Guitar, movie—see BEAUTY (102).

Johnsey, Clair and Debbie—see CHAMP VI.

Johnson, President Lyndon B.—see BLACK JACK (140).

Johnston, General Albert—see FIRE-EATER.

Johnston, General Joseph—see FANNIE.

607. JOHNSTOWN—The 1939 Kentucky Derby winner, a bay colt.

608. JOKER—Jingles P. Jones' horse in the 1952, 1957–1958 television show "Wild Bill Hickok." Jingles was U.S. Marshal James Butler ("Wild Bill") Hickok's partner.

Jondalar—see RACER.

Jones, Buck—see SILVER (1071), WHITE EAGLE.

Jones, Jingle P.—see JOKER.

609. JORDAN—An aged white Welsh cob that appeared dozens of times at the Metropolitan Opera in the 1960s and 1970s. When groomed for his appearances, he would be sprayed with the same kind of cologne used by the prima donna of the opera.

Jorrocks, John—see ARTERXERXES, XERXES.

Joseph, Chief—see EBENEZER (390).

Jouett, Jack—see PRINCE CHARLIE, SALLIE.

Journey Back to Oz, movie—see WOODENHEAD.

610. JUDAS—White horse with roan spots that was used in a carnival diving act around 1924. Sonora Carver rode the horse off a 40-foot tower into an 11-foot tank of water. They had to stop using the horse when he began diving cross-wise instead of straight into the water.

611. JUDGE HIMES—The 1903 Kentucky Derby winner, a chestnut colt.

612. JUDY—Mattie's father's horse in Charles Portis's book, *True Grit.*

613. JUMBO—A big bay gelding owned by Lederle Laboratories. JUMBO gave blood for tetanus antitoxin and pneumonia antiserum from 1929 to 1940. He died in 1944, and a plaque was erected in memory of his service to humanity.

614. JUMPER—The mule belonging to the Coates family in the 1957 movie, *Old Yeller,* based on the book by Fred Gipson.

615. JUNIOR—Glen Campbell's mount on the cover of the *Rhinestone Cowboy* record album.

616. JUPITER—One of the great Belgian sires.

617. JUSTIN MORGAN—The foundation sire of the Morgan breed, thought to be sired by TRUE BRITON, also known as BEAUTIFUL BAY, out of the WILDAIR MARE in the early 1790s. Some say his sire was YOUNG BULROCK, but most say TRUE BRITON. JUSTIN MORGAN was a 14-hand, 950-pound dark bay with black legs, mane, and tail that could work like a draft horse and race like a Throughbred. He was later named after his owner, Justin Morgan, who called him LITTLE BUB first, then FIGURE. His story is told in Marguerite Henry's book, *Justin Morgan Had a Horse.* After his owner's death, the horse was sold several times. President James Monroe once rode him. JUSTIN MORGAN died in the 1820s of a neglected kick injury, and Colonel Joseph Battell began actively promoting and preserving the Morgan horse breed in 1894. One of his well-known grandsons was VERMONT BLACK HAWK.

Justin Morgan Had a Horse, book—see EBENEZER (389), JUSTIN MORGAN, LITTLE BUB.

618. KADETT—A great dressage horse ridden by Jennie Loriston-Clarke.

619. KALKIN—Vishnu the Preserver's white horse in Hinduism.

Kalney, Francis, author—see GITANA, OSOSO.

620. KANGAROO—One of Union General Ulysses S. Grant's horses during the Civil War, an ugly raw-boned Thoroughbred that Grant rescued and valued highly as a war-horse.

THE KANGAROO HORSE—see PHAR LAP.

Kansas City Chiefs—see WAR PAINT (1259).

621. KANTHAKA—One of Buddha's horses, a white stallion. Buddha was the founder of the Buddhist religion.

622. KATIE—Emmett Dalton's first horse, it had previously belonged to Jesse James.

623. KAUAI KING—The 1966 Kentucky Derby winner, a brown colt.

Kearny, General Philip—see BAYARD (97), DECATUR, MONMOUTH, MOSCOW.

624. KEEN—One of Hilda Gurney's international dressage horses.

Kellogg, William—see OLD SPOT (857).

Kelly, Grace—see BABA.

625. KELSO—A dark Thoroughbred racehorse gelding with two white socks that was named Horse of the Year each

year from 1960 to 1964. He was descended from MESSENGER and was one of the richest racehorses ever, winning $1,977,896. He retired at age 9 and was retrained in dressage and jumping. He retired from that at age 17.

Kennedy, Caroline—see LEPRECHAUN, MACARONI, TEX.

Kennedy, Jacqueline—see DANSEUSE, SARDAR.

Kennedy, President John F.—see BLACK JACK (140).

Kennedy, John, Jr.—see LEPRECHAUN, TEX.

626. KENTUCKY—A tireless bay horse used by Confederate president Jefferson Davis.

Keogh, Captain Myles—see COMANCHE (280), PADDY.

627. KHARTOUM—A racehorse worth $600,000 that is beheaded in the movie *The Godfather.*

628. KICKUMS—A mean horse in R.D. Blackmore's book *Lorna Doone.*

629. KIDRON—One of General John Pershing's horses, a chestnut that he rode in parades in 1919.

The Killing, movie—see RED LIGHTNING.

Kilpatrick, General Judson—see BEPPO, OLD SPOT (856).

630. KINCSEM—A Hungarian race mare that was unbeaten in 54 races between 1877 and 1880. She was a lopeared and ewe-necked filly that always started late but always won. Her name means "my treasure" in Hungarian. She raced till the age of 5 when she was kicked, and

then retired to be a successful broodmare. She died at age 14 in 1888, and all of Hungary mourned her death.

631. KING—Velvet Brown's horse in the television show, "National Velvet," 1960–1962. KING was short for **BLAZE KING.**

632. KING—The wild stallion in Glenn Balch's children's books about Ken and Dixie Darby in Idaho.

633. KING—A Quarter Horse sire that died in 1958. His get excelled in racing, showing, and cutting.

634. KING—Bill Cody's white horse in early western movies.

KING CHARLES—see THE PIE (907).

635. KING COTTON—A white Saddlebred stallion that played in the 1960 movie, *Pepe* and was owned and trained by Ralph McCutcheon.

636. KING JOHN—The gray Arabian stallion ridden by Marlene Dietrich in the 1934 movie, *The Scarlet Empress.*

King of the Wind—see THE GODOLPHIN BARB, SHAM.

637. KING PHILIP—The large dark gray gelding ridden by Nathan Bedford Forrest, a Confederate soldier during the Civil War. Forrest was involved in the beginnings of the original Ku Klux Klan.

King Solomon's Horses—see BALA.

638. KINGMAN—The 1891 Kentucky Derby winner, a bay colt.

639. KINGSTON—A racehorse that made 74 starts and never finished out of the money.

Kipling, Rudyard, author—see KITTIWYNK, THE MALTESE CAT.

640. KIT—A brown mare that belonged to President Garfield's daughter Molly. KIT's sidesaddle slipped one day while Molly was riding, and she was dragged by the stirrup. She was unhurt but never rode again.

641. KITTIWYNK—One of the polo team horses in the Rudyard Kipling story, "The Maltese Cat," about polo from the horse's point of view.

642. KLATAWAH—A lively sorrel Thoroughbred gelding that was used in a carnival diving act from around 1924 to 1931. Sonora Carver rode him off a 40-foot tower into an 11-foot tank of water. KLATAWAH was a ham and loved applause, but was also a very dependable diver, despite being a Thoroughbred. Name means "go away."

Klimke, Reiner—see AHLERICH, MEHMED.

643. KLITSCHKA—Trumpeter Wettstein's mount in the Civil War, a small iron-gray mare. Most trumpeters' horses were gray so that they could be seen easily for ordering trumpet calls. KLITSCHKA and Wettstein were trumpeters for Union Colonel George Waring.

644. KLUGE HANS—One of several horses owned and trained by Karl Krall in Elberfeld, Germany, in the late 1800s and early 1900s that could do mathematics. Also called CLEVER HANS or CLEVER JACK. Scientists could find no fraud in the demonstration. See also BERTO.

645. KNIGHT—Rod Cameron's palomino horse in early western movies.

KNOTHER—see ROYAL STUDENT.

646. KOKO—Rex Allen's chestnut horse in western movies in the 1930s and 1940s.

647. KOSMOS—One of Hartwig Steeken's successful show jumpers.

Krall, Karl—see BERTO, KLUGE HANS, MUHAMED, ZARIF.

648. KREPYSH—A Russian trotter that was shot in 1919 for being a "bourgeois" horse. His winnings had totaled nearly $100,000.

Ku Klux Klan—see KING PHILIP.

Kubie, Nora Benjamin, author—see BALA.

649. KUHAYLAH—A wild mare in Arab legend that Ishmael saw while hunting. An angel came to Ishmael and said that the horse was a gift from Allah and would become a treasure to Arabs as the Arabian breed of horses.

Kulhwch—see DU.

Kurma—see UCCAIHSRAVAS.

650. KYRAT—A chestnut Arabian horse with four white socks in Henry Wadsworth Longfellow's poem, "The Leap of Roushan Beg." KYRAT makes a huge leap in order to save Roushan the Robber from being caught.

651. LAD'S VANDY—The first Appaloosa horse owned by television star James Brolin, she was a roan mare with sorrel spots.

652. LADY—The brown trotting mare in the 1956 movie *The Friendly Persuasion*, based on the book by Jessamyn West. The mare was owned by Quaker Jess Birdwell

and would not be passed by other horses. Jess had traded his slower horse RED ROVER for LADY.

653. LADY MARGRAVE—The tall, long-striding chestnut mare ridden by Confederate General Jeb Stuart during the Civil War. The mare was captured by Union soldiers.

654. LADY SUFFOLK—The first trotter to break the 2:30 mile, a gray mare foaled in 1833 and named for the New York county in which she was born and raced. The song "The Old Gray Mare, She Ain't What She Used to Be" is about her. She was rescued from pulling a butcher's cart in 1837 to become a harness-racing horse.

Ladyhawke, movie—see GOLIATH.

655. LAILA—Lady Hester Stanhope's chestnut Thorough-bred mare while in Arabia. Lady Stanhope traveled all over Arabia in the early 1800s.

656. THE LAMB—Won the Grand National Steeplechase in 1868 and 1871 and was the smallest horse to do so.

657. LAMPON—One of Buddha's horses, a white stallion. Name means "shining like a lamp."

658. LAMPOS—One of the horses belonging to Helios, the sun god in classical mythology.

659. LAMPUS—One of Hector's chariot horses in Homer's *Iliad.*

660. LAMPUS—One of the horses that drew the chariot of Eos, goddess of the dawn.

661. LAMRI—One of the horses belonging to the legendary King Arthur, a mare whose name means the "curveter."

Lane, Allan ("Rocky")—see BLACKJACK, MR. ED (777).

"Laredo," television show—see BUTTERMILK (214), CACTUS.

LaRue, Al ("Lash")—see RUSH.

"Lassie," television show—see DOMINO (361).

The Last Outlaw, movie—see FLASH (438).

The Law of the Wild, movie—see REX (973).

Lawrence, D.H., author—see AARON, ST. MAWR.

662. LAWRIN—The 1938 Kentucky Derby winner, a brown colt. His jockey was Eddie Arcaro, who has ridden five Kentucky Derby winners.

Lawson, Robert, author—see SCHEHERAZADE.

"The Leap of Roushan Beg," poem—see KYRAT.

Lederle Laboratories—see JUMBO.

Lee, General Fitzhugh—see NELLIE GRAY.

Lee, Henry ("Light-Horse" Harry)—see MAGNOLIA.

Lee, Robert E.—see AJAX, BROWN ROAN, CREOLE, GRACE DARLING, JIM (599), LUCY LONG, RICHMOND, SANTA ANNA, TRAVELLER (1203).

663. LEGAL TENDER—One of several American Saddle Horses that President Ulysses S. Grant exhibited at the 1871 St. Louis Fair.

The Legend of Sleepy Hollow—see GUNPOWDER, DAREDEVIL.

664. LEGENDAIRE—A racehorse that had a psychiatrist, Byron Hendricks.

665. LEGIONARIO—A well-known gray Andalusian horse.

666. LEGS—A big bay gelding rope horse ridden by cowboy Jake McClure in the 1920s and 1930s. McClure revolutionized the rodeo sport of calf roping. LEGS died in 1937.

667. LEO JR.—The real name of Dale Robertson's Quarter Horse in the television show, "Tales of Wells Fargo."

668. LEONATUS—The 1883 Kentucky Derby winner, a bay colt.

669. LEOPARD—An Arabian stallion that belonged to General Ulysses S. Grant.

670. LEOPARDO III—A white Andalusian stallion featured in photographer Robert Vavra's 1989 book, *Vavra's Horses,* as one of the world's ten most beautiful equines.

671. LEOPOLD—A charger used by Queen Victoria in 1837 to review her troops.

672. LEPRECHAUN—Caroline and John Kennedy, Jr.'s pet pony while their father was president of the United States.

673. LETAN—One of roper, actor, and entertainer Will Rogers' movie horses, an Arabian that was ridden in the movie, *The Texas Steer.*

LET'S MERGE—see RISING STAR.

Lewis, C.S. (Clive Staples), author—see BREE, FLEDGE, HWIN, STRAWBERRY.

Lewis, Jerry—see MY SHEBA.

Lewis, Oliver—see ARISTIDES.

674. LEXINGTON—One of George Washington's white war-horses, which died in the Battle of Monmouth in 1778. There is a painting by John Trumbull of Washington on LEXINGTON.

675. LEXINGTON—Union General William Tecumseh Sherman's Kentucky Thoroughbred horse, which he rode during the Civil War. Sherman is famous for saying, "War is hell." LEXINGTON survived the war in good shape, and Sherman rode him in the final review of his army in Washington after the war.

676. LEXINGTON—The winner of the Great Post Stakes in 1854, a bay with four white socks. Former President Millard Fillmore attended the race, and Currier and Ives made a print of the racehorse.

677. LIEUTENANT GIBSON—The 1900 Kentucky Derby winner, a bay colt.

"The Life and Legend of Wyatt Earp," television show—see CANDY.

"The Life and Times of Grizzly Adams," television show—see NUMBER 7.

"Life with Snarkey Parker," television show—see HEATHCLIFFE.

678. LIGHTNING—A pony in Miram E. Mason's book *A Pony Called Lightning.*

679. LIGHTNING—The racehorse in the story and movie, *The Reivers,* by William Faulkner. LIGHTNING was played in the movie by a horse called MARAUDER.

680. LIGHTNING—One of the horses ridden by Tim Holt in western movies.

Lightning—see WHITE CLOUD (1269).

681. LIMIRICK PRIDE—A horse in Donn Byrne's book *Destiny Bay*.

Lincoln, President Abraham—see BOB, EBONY (391), UNKNOWN HORSE (1240).

682. LINDEN TREE—An Arabian stallion that belonged to General Ulysses S. Grant.

683. LINDY—The chestnut Tennessee Walker that was one of the horses to play Gene Autry's horse in the 1950 TV show "The Adventures of Champion." LINDY was born the day Lindbergh completed his New York to Paris flight in 1927.

684. LISABETH—A movie pack mule owned by William S. Hart that was devoted to Hart's movie horse FRITZ.

685. THE LITHUANIAN—A horse from Lithuania in Rudolph Erich Raspe's book, *The Travels of Baron Munchausen*.

Little Beaver—see PAPOOSE.

Little Big Horn, Battle of—see COMANCHE (280), LITTLE SCOUT'S PAINT HORSE, VIC.

686. LITTLE BIT—One of Nancy Reagan's horses.

687. LITTLE BLACKIE—The horse ridden by 14-year-old Mattie Ross in the 1969 movie, *True Grit*, based on the book by Charles Portis.

LITTLE BUB—see JUSTIN MORGAN.

Little Don Pedro—see CHICKO.

The Little Horse—see WHITE STAR.

"Little House on the Prairie," television show—see PATTY, PET (893).

LITTLE JEFF—see JEFF DAVIS.

688. LITTLE JOHN—An Appaloosa movie horse owned and trained by Slim Pickens. LITTLE JOHN nips Gregory Peck in the movie *The Big Country.*

689. LITTLE MAN—President Ronald Reagan's favorite riding horse, a Thoroughbred gelding he raised from a colt.

690. LITTLE SCOUT'S PAINT HORSE—Believed to be one of the two survivors of Custer's Last Stand at Little Big Horn. The horse wandered into an Arikara Indian village several days after the battle.

LITTLE SORREL—see OLD SORREL.

691. LITTLE SQUIRE—A 13.2-hand Connemara pony that was the U.S. Open Jumping Champion in the 1930s.

692. LITTLE WHITE STAR—A pony in Dorothy Clewes' book *The Old Pony.*

The Littlest Outlaw, movie—see CONQUISTADOR (286).

Livingston, Bob—see STARLIGHT (1121).

693. LIZZIE—The high-strung chestnut mare in Anna Sewell's book, *Black Beauty.*

Llewellyn, Colonel Harry M.—see FOXHUNTER.

694. LOCHNAGAR—A Highland pony ridden by Queen Victoria.

695. LOCO—Pancho's palomino horse in the 1951 television show, "The Cisco Kid." Pancho was played by Leo Carrillo and was the Cisco Kid's partner.

696. LOGAN—A racehorse foaled in 1888 that ran 388 races (a record number of starts for that date) and won 76.

Logan, John—see BLACK JACK (141).

Loki—see SLEIPNIR.

London, Jack—see NEUADD HILLSIDE, WASHOE BAN.

"The Lone Ranger," man, television show, movies, comic books—see SCOUT (1040), SILVER (1069), SILVER CHIEF, SILVER KING (1076), SYLVAAN, VICTOR.

Lone Star, movie—see BEAUTY (102).

"The Loner," television show—see REX (976).

Long, Loula—see REVELATION.

Longden, Johnny—see FLEET DRIVER.

Longfellow, Henry Wadsworth, poet—see KYRAT.

Longstreet, Lieutenant General James—see HERO (542).

697. LOOKOUT—The 1893 Kentucky Derby winner, a chestnut colt.

698. LOOKOUT—Union General Joseph Hooker's charger in the Civil War, named in honor of the Battle of Lookout Mountain. A 17-hand son of Mambrino, LOOKOUT could have been a harness-racing trotter.

699. LORD APPLETON—A bay Morgan stallion featured in photographer Robert Vavra's 1989 book, *Vavra's Horses* as one of the world's ten most beautiful equines.

700. LORD MURPHY—The 1879 Kentucky Derby winner, a bay colt.

Lord of the Rings, book—see SHADOWFAX, SNOW-MANE.

Loriston-Clarke, Jennie—see KADETT.

Lorna Doone, book—see KICKUMS, WINNIE.

701. LOTTERY—Winner of the 1839 Grand National Steeplechase.

702. LOUISA—The racehorse ridden to victory by Alicia Thornton in a match race in 1805. Mrs. Thornton always dressed very stylishly when racing her horses.

703. LUCKY—Packy's horse in the television show "Fury," 1955–1966. Packy was Joey Newton's friend.

704. LUCKY DEBONAIR—The 1965 Kentucky Derby winner, a bay colt.

705. LUCY—Confederate General George Pickett's chestnut Thoroughbred mare in the Civil War.

706. LUCY LONG—A 15-hand, gentle sorrel mare ridden by Confederate General Robert E. Lee during the Civil War, a gift from Jeb Stuart. Lee called her MISS LUCY. She had a fast walk and an easy canter but not enough stamina to be used exclusively in the war. One story says she broke her picket line to mate with a stallion and had to be sent back to the farm, while another said she broke down in battle. She was lost for several years, but Lee found her later and kept her. LUCY LONG died in 1891 at age 39.

Ludington, Sybil—see UNKNOWN HORSE (1239).

Ludwig II, King of Bavaria—see COSA RARA.

707. LULU—Lady Hester Stanhope's gray Thoroughbred mare while traveling all over Arabia in the early 1800s.

Lundy, Peter—see SAN DOMINGO.

708. LUNO—The winged stallion in Mighty Mouse cartoons.

709. LYARD—A horse belonging to King Richard I (the Lion-hearted), a gray Arabian. Name means "gray."

710. MA—The horse of the sun in Chinese mythology.

711. MACARONI—Caroline Kennedy's favorite pony when her father John F. Kennedy was president.

MacArthur, General Douglas—see BLACK JACK (140).

712. MACBETH II—The 1888 Kentucky Derby winner, a brown gelding.

MacDonald, George, author—see DIAMOND.

Macken, Eddie—see BOOMERANG, PELE.

Mad Jack—see NUMBER 7.

713. MADAME LA REALE—The favorite horse of Mary, Queen of Scots, in the 1500s.

714. MAESTOSO—One of the founding sires of the famous Lippizan horses of the Spanish Riding School.

715. MAGGIE—An old gray mare in the Robert Burns' poem "Tam O'Shanter," based on an old Scottish tale. The mare was being ridden home from a tavern one stormy night by Tam O'Shanter when he saw the devil dancing with witches in the church. Tam laughed at them, and the witches chased him and pulled the tail off his mare. Some versions name the horse MEG.

716. MAGGIE—An old horse in Robert Burns' poem "The Auld Farmer's New Year Morning Salutation to his

Auld Mare Maggie," about an old farmer feeding corn to an old mare on New Year's morning.

The Magician's Nephew—see FLEDGE.

717. MAGNIFIQUE—The white horse that carries Beauty to and from the Beast in Cocteau's film *Beauty and the Beast*.

718. MAGNOLIA—One of George Washington's favorite Thoroughbred stallions in 1785. He put the horse in a race against Thomas Jefferson's roan colt in 1788, and MAGNOLIA lost. Washington later traded the horse for land. "Light-Horse" Harry Lee, an American general during the Revolution, later owned the horse.

719. MAHMOUD—Thoroughbred racehorse foaled in 1933 that belonged to the Aga Khan. He won an English Derby in the fastest time ever. He was retired in 1940 and went to stud in the United States.

720. MAHOMET—One of the four horses that Eadweard Muybridge photographed in the 1870s to show that all four feet of a horse leave the ground during the gallop.

Mahomet—see AL BORAK.

Mahoney, Jock—see RAWHIDE.

721. MAHUBAH—The successful broodmare that was the dam of MAN O'WAR, and whose Arab name means "good greetings," or "good fortune." MAN O'WAR got her long stride and sweet temperament.

722. MAJESTIC PRINCE—The 1969 Kentucky Derby winner, a chestnut colt. His jockey was Bill Hartack, who has ridden five Kentucky Derby winners. MAJES-TIC PRINCE was undefeated after his 1969 win.

723. MAJOR—The old horse that was turned into a coach-man for Cinderella's carriage in one version of the Cinderella tale.

724. MAJOR—Union General Ambrose Burnside's favorite war-horse in the Civil War. MAJOR lived to be about 30 years old.

725. MAJOR TREAT—A placid 10-year-old hunter that was used as a calming influence in the training of MAN O'WAR.

Maktoum, Hamdal al—see NASHWAN.

Malcuidant—see SALT PERDU.

726. THE MALTESE CAT—One of the polo ponies in Rudyard Kipling's story, "The Maltese Cat," about a polo game told from the horse's point of view.

"The Maltese Cat," story—see KITTIWYNK, THE MALTESE CAT.

727. MAMBRINO—A foundation sire of the gaited horse and the sire of MESSENGER.

"The Man from Snowy River," poem—see REGRET (970).

728. MAN O'WAR—A famous chestnut stallion foaled in 1917, owned by Samuel Riddle, and bred by August Belmont. MAN O' WAR was one of the greatest racehorses ever, and his nickname was BIG RED. His sire was FAIR PLAY and his dam was MAHUBAH. His pedigree could be traced back to the Godolphin Arabian. He was difficult to train and disliked being saddled. MAN O'WAR won both the Preakness and the Belmont in 1920 and won a match race against JOHN P. GRIER the same year. He did not run in the Kentucky Derby as it was not then so highly regarded as

it is now. He sired many famous racehorses, such as WAR ADMIRAL. His name was originally MY MAN O'WAR, but the auctioneer dropped the "My" when he was auctioned off as a yearling for $5,000. He lost only one race, to UPSET in 1919. He had been mishandled at the barrier, and when the race started he was not facing the right way. MAN O'WAR damaged a tendon and retired in 1921. He was visited by many people before he died of colic at age 26 in November 1947, less than one month after his devoted groom Will Harbut died. He was originally buried at Faraway Farms, but his remains were moved in 1976.

Manannan—see ENBARR.

729. MANCHA—An Argentine Criollo pony ridden, along with GATO, by Aime F. Tschiffely from Buenos Aires, Argentina, to Washington D.C., a 2½-year (1925–1927) trip of nearly 10,000 miles. MANCHA was 16 years old and wild when the trip started. He was a red and white skewbald whose name means "stained." Tschiffely took the journey to show the world what a hardy breed the Criollos were. MANCHA was hit by a car and almost got a parking ticket during the trip. He died in 1947 at age 40; his body is on exhibit at the Colonial Museum in Lujan near Buenos Aires.

Mani—see ALSVIDER.

730. MANICOU—The first racehorse to carry the Queen Mother's racing colors.

731. MANIFESTO—Racehorse that won the 1897 and 1899 Grand National Steeplechase.

732. MANITOU—Theodore Roosevelt's horse during his ranching days.

733. MANUEL—The 1899 Kentucky Derby winner, a bay colt, who won out of a field of five horses.

MARAUDER—see LIGHTNING (679).

734. MARENGO—Napoleon Bonaparte's favorite light-colored war-horse. The stallion was a gray or white Arabian imported from Egypt as a 6-year-old in 1799. He was a small horse, 14.1 hands. Napoleon named the stallion in honor of the Battle of Marengo, a French victory, and rode him for part of the battle of Waterloo in 1815 when MARENGO was 22 years old. One story says that when MARENGO received a hip wound, Napoleon changed horses, and that Napoleon escaped but MARENGO was captured by the British. MARENGO outlived Napoleon by eight years and died in the 1830s in his thirties. His skeleton is mounted as a military trophy at Whitehall in London. A snuffbox was made out of one of his hooves.

735. THE MARES OF DIOMEDES—Four mares that belonged to Diomedes, the king of the Bistones in Thrace, who were said to eat human flesh. The eighth labor of Hercules was to destroy them. Some classical myths say that Hercules did not destroy them, but tamed them. Others say that they escaped.

736. MARIE—One of Napoleon Bonaparte's favorite white war-horses.

737. MARK—One of the Budweiser Clydesdale geldings from the eight-horse hitch that toured the fourteen western states.

Marko, King of Serbia—see SHARATZ.

738. MARKY—A pinto stallion that fought with REX in movie scenes. One scene of them fighting was sold many times for different movies.

Marmion, poem—see BEVIS.

739. MARMIORE—Villain Grandoigne's swift horse in the epic poem *The Song of Roland.*

Marnie, movie—see FORIO.

740. MAROCCO—One of the first performing horses, during the Elizabethan period. The bay gelding could dance on his hind legs and answer questions with a nod or shake of his head. He and his master Thomas Banks were accused of performing magic and the pope ordered that they be burned to death. Banks escaped but it is not known if MAROCCO did. Shakespeare referred to him once.

741. MARS—One of Messala's Arabian chariot horses in Lew Wallace's book, *Ben-Hur.*

Mars—see DEIMOS, PHOBOS.

742. MARSALA—Italian patriot Giuseppe Garibaldi's horse in the 1800s, a gray mare.

743. MARSE ROBERT—The horse that pulled the buckboard driven by Rhett Butler in the 1939 movie *Gone with the Wind* during the burning of Atlanta. MARSE ROBERT was a vernacular reference to General Robert E. Lee.

744. MARSHAL—Marshal Matt Dillon's horse's real name in the television show, "Gunsmoke," 1955–1975. MARSHAL's television name was BUCK.

Marsilon—see GAIGNUN.

745. MARTHA—Cartoon horse Quick Draw McGraw's mother in the TV cartoon show, "The Quick Draw McGraw Show."

Martin, Dean—see MY SHEBA.

Marty—see SKYROCKET.

Marvel, Professor—see SYLVESTER (1156).

Marvin, Lee—see SMOKEY.

Marx, Harpo—see HI HAT.

Mary, Queen of Scots—see MADAME LA REALE, ROSABELLA.

746. MARYE—Confederate General John Gordon's beautiful Thoroughbred war-horse in the Civil War. MARYE was good in battle and was never wounded. Gordon's wife rode MARYE as a saddle horse whenever she came to visit him during the war.

747. MARYLAND—A big bay horse ridden by Confederate General Jeb Stuart during the Civil War. The gelding had been given to him by a female admirer.

"M*A*S*H," television show—see PEGASUS (887), SOPHIE.

Mason, Miram E., author—see LIGHTNING (678), WHITE CLOUD (1269).

748. MATCHEM—A grandson of THE GODOLPHIN BARB, foaled in 1748. He was a foundation sire of the Thoroughbred horse.

749. MAUD—A mule in the comic strip, "And Her Name Was Maud."

750. MAUD—A California horse living around 1905 whose mane measured 18 feet.

751. MAUD S—A mare that set the mile trotting record as a 10-year-old in the late 1800s and died in 1900.

May, Charles—see BLACK TOM.

Maynard, Ken—see TARZAN.

Maynard, Kermit ("Tex")—see ROCKY.

752. MAX—Union Colonel George Waring's war-horse in the Civil War. The 16-hand dark bay jumper carried Waring through many battles with courage and endurance.

McCaffrey, Anne, author—see MISTER ED (778).

McCain, Lucas—see RAZOR.

McCain, Mark—see BLUE BOY.

McCarthy, Clem—see FAULTLESS, JET PILOT.

McClellan, General George B.—see BURNS, DANIEL WEBSTER.

McClure, Jake—see LEGS, SILVER (1072).

McCool, Finn of the Fair Hair—see THE MEAN MARE.

McCoy, Tim—see ACE (9), BARON (90), MIDNIGHT (767), PAL (869), STARLIGHT (1121).

McCrea, Joel—see DOLLAR (357), STEEL.

McCutcheon, Ralph—see DICE, FURY (466), FURY JR., KING COTTON.

McDowell, Dr. Ephraim—see UNKNOWN HORSE (1227).

753. MCKINLEY—William F. ("Buffalo Bill") Cody's last white show horse. He was not the white horse at Cody's funeral in 1917—that was a livery stable horse.

McLaughlin, Ken—see FLICKA.

McQueen, Steve—see RINGO.

McTaggart, Lieutenant Colonel Maxwell Fielding—see OZONE.

Meade, General George—see BALDY (80).

754. THE MEAN MARE—A skinny, mean yellow mare in Irish legend that is really a beautiful, smooth white mare belonging to Abartha (The Hard Servant). Fourteen men, including Finn McCool of the Fair Hair, tried to ride her at one time to cure her of her meanness and were transported to the Land-Under-Wave.

755. MEDLEY—A descendant of MESSENGER.

Meet Me in St. Louis, movie—see ROBIN.

MEG—see MAGGIE (715).

756. MEHEYL—An Arabian horse belonging to director Mike Nichols.

757. MEHMED—A successful dressage horse ridden by Reiner Klimke.

758. MENIK—One of the horses of the sun, along with BENIK, ENIK, and SENIK, in Persian mythology.

The Merchant of Venice, play—see DOBBIN.

759. MERIDIAN—The 1911 Kentucky Derby winner, a bay colt.

760. MERRY LEGS F-4—The foundation mare of the Tennessee Walking Horse breed.

761. MERRYLEGS—The fat gray pony from BLACK BEAUTY's early days in Anna Sewell's book, *Black Beauty.*

762. MESROUR—Edward Rochester's black horse in Charlotte Bronte's book, *Jane Eyre.*

Messala—see EROS, MARS.

763. MESSENGER—A big gray English Thoroughbred stallion that came to America in 1788, and was also called IMPORTED MESSENGER. He was sired by MAMBRINO and was a descendant of THE DARLEY ARABIAN. He was the grandsire of THE AMERICAN ECLIPSE and the foundation sire for most harness-racing horses. He died in 1808.

Metropolitan Opera—see JORDAN.

MEXICAN MAN O'WAR—see ZANATON.

Mickey Mouse cartoons—see HORACE HORSECOLLAR.

"The Mickey Mouse Club," television show—see DYNAMITE, SAILOR, SKYROCKET.

764. MIDDLEGROUND—The 1950 Kentucky Derby winner, a chestnut colt.

765. MIDNIGHT—A big, heavy, strong black rodeo bucking horse from the 1930s. He was foaled in Alberta, Canada, and was used as a pleasure horse until he started bucking. After U.S. rodeo promoters bought him, he became the World's Champion Bucking Horse and received a jewel-studded feed bag. His body is now buried at the Cowboy Hall of Fame in Oklahoma City.

766. MIDNIGHT—A horse that doubled for CASS OLE when he played THE BLACK in the 1983 movie *The Black Stallion Returns.*

767. MIDNIGHT—The black stallion ridden by Tim McCoy in early western movies.

768. MIDNIGHT STAR—A champion 5-gaited gelding.

THE MIGHTY ATOM—see WAR ADMIRAL.

"Mighty Mouse," cartoon—see LUNO.

769. MIKE—Actor George O'Brien's black horse in early western movies.

Miles, Nelson—see EXCELSIOR.

770. MILL REEF—A racehorse in the 1970s.

Miller, Jeff—see DOMINO (361).

Millhouse, Frog—see NELLIE (815), RING EYE.

Mills, Hayley—see ARABELLE, BEAUTY (100).

Milne, A.A., author—see EEYORE.

771. MINORU—A racehorse that won the English Derby in 1909 carrying the colors of King Edward VII of England.

The Misfits, movie—see BOOTS.

772. MISS ADA—The Brown's elderly pink roan pony mare in Enid Bagnold's book *National Velvet.*

MISS LUCY—see LUCY LONG.

773. MISS MOBRAY—A mare that won the 1852 Grand National Steeplechase, the second mare ever to win that race.

774. MISS REX—A 15.2-hand gray high-school and 5-gaited American Saddle Horse mare owned and trained by Tom Bass, a black horseman, in the 1890s. President Grover Cleveland once admired her at a show.

775. MISS TURNER—A Welsh race mare that ran against the English RATTLER in the first international horse race in England in 1829.

MIST-O-SHOT—see MISTY (785).

776. MR. DINKUM—Prince Andrew's first horse as a child.

777. MR. ED.—The talking palomino, half-American Saddlebred Horse in the television show "Mr. Ed," 1960–1966. He belonged to Wilber and Carol Post and his voice was done by Allan ("Rocky") Lane.

778. MISTER ED—Science fiction writer Anne McCaffrey's first horse, a gray gelding.

MR. LONGTAIL—see WHIRLAWAY.

779. MR. NICKERSON—Racehorse that had a heart attack and died in the middle of the televised 1990 Breeders' Cup Sprint.

780. MR. POTTS—A stubborn family mule that was trained to be 5-gaited by young Tom Bass, a black horseman, in the 1880s.

Mr. Revere and I, book—see SCHEHERAZADE.

781. MR. RYTHM—A chestnut Saddlebred gelding, trained by Darrel Wallen, that could do 56 tricks, including walking on his hind legs, cantering sideways, and bowing. After only one month of training he could do 35 tricks. His name originally was BORN FREE, and was changed to MR. RYTHM when his act was taken on the road.

782. MR. SAN PEPPY—A successful cutting horse.

MR. WALTER K—see DRUMS IN THE NIGHT.

783. MRS. JAMES—A 9-year-old gray polo pony mare, 15 hands, one of five horses that Velvet Brown inherited from Mr. Cellini in Enid Bagnold's book, *National Velvet.*

784. MISTY—The Chincoteague pony that Paul and Maureen Beebe owned in Marguerite Henry's book, *Misty of Chincoteague.* MISTY later had the foal STORMY in the book *Stormy, Misty's Foal.* The stories were based on a real pony's life. MISTY's story was told in the 1961 movie, *Misty,* in which MISTY was played by three different ponies.

785. MISTY—A well-known black Thoroughbred stallion that starred in 70 movies. MIST-O-SHOT was his racetrack name. He played BANNER in the movies *My Friend Flicka* and *Thunderhead,* and was a wild horse in the movie *Duel in the Sun* starring Gregory Peck.

786. MISTY GIRL—Victoria Barkley's horse in the television show "The Big Valley."

Misty of Chincoteague, book—see BLACK COMET, MISTY (784), PHANTOM (897), PIED PIPER.

Mix, Tom—see OLD BLUE (845), TONY, TONY JR.

Mobil Oil Company—see PEGASUS (888).

Mohammed—see AL BORAK.

787. MOHAMMED'S TEN HORSES—Ten obedient horses that constituted the foundation of the Prophet Strain of horses.

788. MOIFAA—A 17-hand, 8-year-old racehorse that was lost overboard in a storm while being transported from New Zealand to England in 1904. He washed up on a deserted island and was found two weeks later. He came

back to win the Grand National Steeplechase in 1904 by eight lengths.

789. MOLLIE—The pretty but foolish white mare in George Orwell's book, *Animal Farm*. She drew Mr. Jones' trap before the Rebellion, but she liked sugar and ribbons and left the farm so she could have them.

790. MONARCH—A horse ridden by Queen Victoria that once shied and unseated her in front of the prime minister.

Mondale, Eleanor—see SUNNY.

Money from Home, movie—see MY SHEBA.

791. MONMOUTH—General Philip Kearny's iron-gray horse that was led during Kearny's funeral procession. MONMOUTH was a veteran of the Mexican War but was too old to be used in the Civil War.

Montana, Monte—see REX (975).

792. MONTE—The black-and-white pinto that artist Charles Russell owned as a child and kept until the horse died of old age.

793. MONTE—The Virginian's horse in Owen Wister's western book, *The Virginian*.

794. MONTROSE—The 1887 Kentucky Derby winner, a bay colt.

795. MONTROSE—A mahogany bay American Saddle Horse stallion in the late 1870s that sired the Rose family of saddlers.

MONTROSE SEA—see REX (976).

Moody, Ralph, author—see SEABISCUIT, SYLPH.

Morgan, John Hunt—see BLACK BESS (134), GLEN-COE.

796. MOROCCO—Was claimed to be the tallest horse in 1908, standing 21.2 hands.

Morrissey, Mick—see ROYAL STUDENT.

797. MORVICH—The 1922 Kentucky Derby winner, a brown colt.

MORZILLO—see EL MORZILLO.

798. MOSCOW—Union General Philip Kearny's white horse during the Civil War.

Mottistone, Lord—see WARRIOR (1261).

799. MUHAMED—One of several horses owned and trained by Karl Krall in Elberfeld, Germany, in the late 1800s and early 1900s that could do mathematics. MUHAMED could calculate cube roots with a sack over his head, as well as add, subtract, multiply, and divide. Scientists could find no fraud in the demonstration. See also KLUGE HANS (644).

Muhammad—see AL BORAK.

Murphy, Michael—see WILDFIRE (1279).

Muses—see PEGASUS (886).

800. MUSON—One of the snow-white horses that William F. ("Buffalo Bill") Cody rode in his Wild West shows.

Mussolini, Benito—see FRU-FRU.

801. MUTT—One of Hoot Gibson's horses in his early western movies in the 1930s.

Muybridge, Eadweard—see ABE EDGINGTON, MA-HOMET, OCCIDENT, SALLIE GARDNER.

My Fair Lady, movie—see DOVER.

My Friend Flicka, book, movie, television show—see BANNER (84), FLICKA, ROCKET, THUNDER-HEAD.

MY MAN O'WAR—see MAN O'WAR.

802. MY MISTAKE—The sorrel racehorse in Edna Ferber's book *Giant.* Jordan buys the horse and falls in love with the previous owner's daughter.

My Pal Trigger, movie—see TRIGGER.

803. MY SHEBA—A winning racehorse in the 1953 Jerry Lewis and Dean Martin movie, *Money from Home.*

804. NANA—The red-gold chestnut filly racehorse in Emile Zola's classic novel *Nana.* NANA had not won before, but was triumphant at France's Grand Prix race in chapter 11. Her owner later committed suicide. The horse was named after a woman in the novel.

805. NAPOLEON—General Winfield Scott's favorite horse during the Civil War. The 18-hand horse survived the war and died at age 30 in 1870.

806. NAPOLEON—The old gray cart horse companion for THE BLACK in Walter Farley's book *The Black Stallion.*

807. NAPOLITANO—One of the founding sires of the famous Lippizan horses of the Spanish Riding School.

808. NASHUA—A Thoroughbred racehorse that won the 2-year-old Champion of the Year Award in 1954 and the 3-year-old award in 1955. He also ran in a match race against SWAPS.

809. NASHWAN—The 1989 Epson Derby winner, a colt owned by Hamdan al-Maktoum. Hamdan is one of four

Maktoum brothers from oil-rich Dubai who have spent millions of dollars on the world's finest blood stock, helping the horse-racing industry but causing prices to become inflated.

810. NASRULLAH—A well-known Thoroughbred sire.

Nathan, Samuel ("Nails")—see RAJAH.

National Velvet, book, movie, television show—see ANGELINA, FANCY, GEORGE, KING (631), MISS ADA, MRS. JAMES, THE PIE (907), SIR PERICLES.

811. NATIVE DANCER—A great racehorse, one of the first to appear on television. The gray horse, also known as THE GRAY GHOST, lost only one race, to DARK STAR, in the 1953 Kentucky Derby.

812. NAUTILLUS—A successful show jumper that was discovered in a riding stable.

Navarre, Captain—see GOLIATH.

813. NEEDLES—The 1956 Kentucky Derby winner, a bay colt.

Neely, Mr.—see ROBIN.

814. NEGRITO—Tex's horse in S.E. Hinton's book, *Tex*. Tex's father stayed away from home so long that Tex's brother had to sell their horses in order to get by. *Tex* is also a 1982 movie in which the horse is called ROWDY.

815. NELLIE—One of Frog Millhouse's horses in movies.

816. NELLIE—Oaky Doaks' horse in the comic strip, "Oaky Doaks."

817. NELLIE—A sway-backed mare that appeared in many Three Stooges movies.

818. NELLIE GRAY—The mare that Confederate General Fitzhugh Lee (Robert E. Lee's nephew) rode in the Civil War. The dapple-gray mare, with a white mane and tail, was killed at the Battle of Winchester.

819. NELSON—A favorite mount of George Washington, a big-boned chestnut gelding with a white face and legs. He was a present from the governor of Virginia, Thomas Nelson, Jr., in 1765. Washington hunted with him for ten years until the war started and then found him to be good in battle. Washington rode him at Valley Forge. After NELSON retired he was called OLD NELSON. NELSON was still alive in 1785 at the age of 23 when a census of Washington's stable showed he had 130 horses. No paintings were done of Nelson.

Nelson, Johnny—see PEPPER.

820. NEUADD HILLSIDE—A Shire stallion that writer Jack London purchased for his model California farm in 1916. The horse died soon after of a sudden illness.

821. NEVELE PRIDE—The dark Standardbred trotter that was the Harness Racing Horse of the Year from 1967 to 1969. The stallion was vicious in the stall but won 57 of his 67 races. Foaled in Pennsylvania in 1965, his name was changed from THANKFUL'S MAJOR to NEVELE PRIDE after his owner's hotel. He was trained by Stanley Dancer and won the Harness Racing Triple Crown in 1968. He broke GREYHOUND's mile record of 1:55.25 in 1969, 31 years after it was set. He was syndicated for $3 million and retired to stud in 1969 as the fastest trotter in history.

822. NEVER MIND II—The steeplechase horse with the record for the slowest winning time for two miles— 11:28, when the normal time would have been 4 minutes. The rest of the field fell or were disqualified, and he was the only horse to finish.

823. NEVER SAY DIE—Won the English Epson Derby in 1954, the first American-bred horse to do so since 1881. His jockey was Lester Piggott.

New Cautionary Tales for Children—see JACK (579), TOM THE POLO PONY.

824. NEW DEAL—A Missouri-bred red bay American Saddle Horse that was presented to President Franklin Roosevelt by friends in Missouri in 1933. The horse had a white star and snip, four white socks, and a good disposition.

825. NEWCOMER—The 14.2-hand brown-and-white pinto mare that was the mascot for the Baltimore Colts football team in the 1970s. She had a filly named GIMME A C.

Newes, Ralph—see FLANAKINS.

Newman, Paul—see HUD.

Newton, Joey—see FURY (466).

826. NIATROSS—A Standardbred harness-racing colt that earned $2,019,213 before retiring from racing in 1981. The bay horse was the first of any breed to win over $2 million in two years of racing. He was the Harness Racing Horse of the Year in 1979 and 1980.

The Nibelungenlied—see GRANI.

Nichols, Mike—see MEHEYL.

827. NICKEL COIN—The racehorse that won the Grand National Steeplechase in 1951 at 40 to 1 odds after being trained on a diet supplement of duck eggs and beer.

828. NICKELS—A 15-hand chestnut gelding rope horse in the 1940s that was foaled in 1937. His rider once gave a calf-roping exhibition on him without a bridle.

829. NIGHTMARE—Casper's ghost horse friend in the animated television show, "Casper the Friendly Ghost."

830. NIJINSKY—A Canadian-bred, Irish-trained racehorse in the 1970s that won the European Triple Crown.

831. NITA—A gray part-mustang mare that pulled a railroad car and raced against "Tom Thumb," the experimental engine car in 1930. NITA won the race, because "Tom Thumb" broke down.

832. NO STRINGS—Nancy Reagan's bay riding horse.

833. NOBS—The big chestnut that carried Dr. Daniel Dove in *The Doctor* by Robert Southey.

834. NONIOS—One of the four black horses belonging to Pluto in classical mythology.

835. NOOR—A successful Irish-bred racehorse.

North, Ricky—see CHAMPION.

836. NORTH SEA—A racehorse ridden by female jockey Robyn Smith in 1973. NORTH SEA was the first major stakes winner ridden by a woman.

837. NORTHERN DANCER—The 1964 Kentucky Derby winner, a bay Canadian colt. He was one of the few Kentucky Derby winners that was not foaled in the United States. His jockey was Bill Hartack, who has ridden five Kentucky Derby winners.

838. NORTHWIND—A stallion in Herbert Ravenel Sass's *The Way of the Wild*.

Nott—see HRIMFAXI.

839. NUGGET—Alan Strang's favorite horse in Peter Shaffer's play, *Equus*. Despite his attachment to NUGGET, Strang blinds him and several other horses. In the play the horses are played by people wearing horse heads and hooves.

840. NUMBER ONE SPY—One of Rodney Jenkins' successful show jumpers.

841. NUMBER 7—Mad Jack's mule in the 1977 television show "The Life and Times of Grizzly Adams."

Numbers 22:21-35, Bible—see BALAAM'S ASS.

842. OAHU—The safe riding horse in Mark Twain's book, *Roughing It*. OAHU had no spirit and an odd canter.

Oakley, Annie—see BUTTERCUP, TARGET.

"Oaky Doaks," comic strip—see NELLIE (816).

O'Brian, Hugh—see CANDY.

O'Brien, George—see MIKE.

843. OCCIDENT—One of the four horses Eadweard Muybridge photographed in the 1870s to show that all four feet of a horse leave the ground during the gallop.

Odin—see SLEIPNIR.

Ogier the Dane—see BROIEFORT.

O'Hara, Mary, author—see BANNER (84), FLICKA, ROCKET, THUNDERHEAD.

Oklahoma!, movie—see BLUE.

Old Billy / 127

844. OLD BILLY—An English horse said to be the oldest on record. He was foaled in 1760 and towed barges until he died in 1822 at the age of 62. His skull is on display in the Manchester Museum.

845. OLD BLUE—Tom Mix's first saddle horse in western movies, a white range horse.

846. OLD BLUE—Actor Dale Robertson's horse in the movie, *Death Valley Days*.

OLD BONES—see EXTERMINATOR.

847. OLD CHARLIE—A dark-colored half-blooded Kentucky horse with a white blaze and two white socks that was ridden by William F. ("Buffalo Bill") Cody in his Wild West shows. Cody bought him in 1873 and called him CHARLIE in his younger years. Cody broke and trained the horse as a 5-year-old and considered him to be a faithful friend. On a bet, Cody once covered 100 miles in less than 10 hours on OLD CHARLIE. Cody took this horse on his tours across America and to Europe to perform for Queen Victoria. OLD CHARLIE died after taking a chill on the ship bringing them home from Europe in the late 1880s. He was buried at sea.

OLD DIAMOND—see DIAMOND.

OLD FOOLER—see H BOMB.

848. OLD FOOLER—An old stubborn horse in the television show, "The Rounders."

"The Old Gray Mare, She Ain't What She Used To Be," song—see LADY SUFFOLK.

OLD IRON HORSE—see SEABISCUIT.

849. OLD KING—The foundation sire of the Albino breed, an Arabian-Morgan cross that helped to develop this type. Albinos are white with brown or blue eyes.

OLD NELSON—see NELSON.

850. OLD PETE—One of Sam Houston's horses in the mid-1800s, a gentle stallion.

The Old Pony—see LITTLE WHITE STAR.

851. OLD ROSEBUD—The 1914 Kentucky Derby winner, a bay gelding.

852. OLD ROWLEY—The favorite stallion of King Charles II of England in the late 1600s.

853. OLD SHORTY—American polo player Thomas Hitchcock's favorite pony. He rode OLD SHORTY in the 1924 International polo championships when OLD SHORTY was 12 years old.

854. OLD SMOKY—One of William F. ("Buffalo Bill") Cody's ranch horses. Gertrude Vanderbilt Whitney made a statue of Cody mounted on OLD SMOKY.

855. OLD SORREL—Confederate General Thomas J. ("Stonewall") Jackson's favorite charger in the Civil War that was a Saddle Horse type and naturally gaited. He was known by several names: FANCY, SORREL, OLD SORREL, and LITTLE SORREL (to distinguish him from a larger sorrel Jackson had). Jackson was killed in 1863 when his own men mistook him for the enemy. When OLD SORREL died, his skeleton was preserved in the Museum of the Virginia Military Institute at Lexington.

856. OLD SPOT—One of Union General Judson Kilpatrick's chargers in the Civil War, a fine Arabian jumper. Kilpatrick rode OLD SPOT in a jumping contest after the war against Confederate General Hampton's BUTLER and lost. OLD SPOT survived many battles and died in 1887 at age 40.

857. OLD SPOT—Breakfast-food pioneer William Kellogg's favorite pony as a child. Later in life, Kellogg raised Arabians.

OLD STEAMBOAT—see STEAMBOAT (1124).

858. OLD WHITEY—General Zachary Taylor's white warhorse that fought in two wars and served under four flags. Taylor got him during the Mexican War from a Mexican officer. He was also called WHITEY. When Taylor became President in 1847, he turned WHITEY out to pasture on the White House lawn. Two years later, OLD WHITEY marched in Taylor's funeral procession. Fourteen years after the Mexican War he was taken by Union soldiers to fight in the Civil War. OLD WHITEY was then around 20 years old. He survived the Civil War and died of old age in retirement.

Old Yeller, movie—see JUMPER.

Oliver, Lieutenant Robert—see DICK (347).

Olivier, Laurence—see BLAUNCHKYNG.

859. OLYMPIA—A Thoroughbred racehorse that won a match race against Quarter Horse champion STELLA MOORE over almost a quarter-mile track in 1949.

860. OMAHA—The 1935 Triple Crown winner, a chestnut colt with a white blaze. The high-strung stallion was also known as the BELAIR BULLET. His sire was the 1930 Triple Crown winner GALLANT FOX. OMAHA, however, was a failure at stud. He died in 1959.

861. OMAR KHAYYAM—The 1917 Kentucky Derby winner, a chestnut colt. He was one of the few Kentucky Derby winners that was not foaled in the United States.

101 Dalmations, movie—see THE CAPTAIN (233).

862. ORELIO—Roderick's loyal white horse in Robert Southey's poem, "Roderick, the Last of the Goths."

Orlando—see BRIGLIADORO.

Orwell, George, author—see BENJAMIN, BOXER, CLOVER, MOLLIE.

O'Shanter, Tam—see MAGGIE (715).

863. OSOSO—The horse in Francis Kalnay's book, *Chacaro, Wild Pony of the Pampas.*

"Our Gang," television show—see DINAH THE MULE.

The Outlaw, movie—see RED.

864. OVER THE TOP—One of MAN O'WAR's famous sons.

865. OZONE—A chestnut mare retrained and ridden by Lieutenant Colonel Maxwell Fielding McTaggart, a famous equestrian theorist and rider. When McTaggart first took the mare on, she was too nervous to do anything, but he developed her into a calm, well-schooled jumper.

Pablito—see CONQUISTADOR.

866. THE PACING WHITE MUSTANG—A legendary wild white stallion claimed to have been seen from the Rio Grande to the Rocky Mountains. One story about the stallion said that a young girl who had been strapped to the back of an old mare following a pioneer wagon had fallen asleep and gotten lost. She saw THE PACING WHITE STALLION, who helped her get back to her family.

Packy—see LUCKY.

867. PADDY—One of Captain Myles Keogh's horses in the U.S. 7th Cavalry, a Thoroughbred he rode on long marches. Keogh saved his other horse, COMANCHE, for military action. Keogh was killed at the Battle of Little Big Horn in 1876.

Paine, Thomas—see BUTTON.

PAINT—see SCOUT (1040).

868. PAL—Dale Evans' first horse, a palomino she rode in rodeo performances with Roy Rogers before their television show began.

869. PAL—One of Tim McCoy's white horses in early western movies in the 1930s.

870. PAL—A brown mule owned by J.E. Campbell of Prineville, Oregon, that saved his owner from a maddened bull's attack in 1931. PAL was awarded the Latham Foundation's Gold Medal for animal heroes.

871. PAL—A golden palomino horse ridden by Gene Autry in early western movies.

Pancho—see LOCO.

Panza, Sancho—see DAPPLE.

Papa's Delicate Condition, movie—see TOSSY.

872. PAPILLON—A fire-breathing horse in Carolingian legend. Name means "butterfly."

Papon, Jim—see STANLEYVILLE STEAMER.

873. PAPOOSE—Indian Little Beaver's pony. Little Beaver was Cowboy Red Ryder's sidekick in comic strips, television, and radio.

874. PARDNER—Al Hoxie's horse in silent western movies.

875. PARDNER—Monte Hale's horse in western movies.

Parker, Snarkey—see HEATHCLIFFE.

876. PAROLE—The winning horse in a three-horse race that both houses of the U.S. Congress voted to attend in 1877 at Pimlico. PAROLE won over TEN BROECK and TOM OCHILTREE. Currier and Ives made a print of the race.

877. PARROT—The 3-year-old racehorse in John Galsworthy's *Caravan: The Assembled Tales of John Galsworthy.* PARROT raced in the short story "Had a Horse."

878. PASSECERF—Gerier's war-horse in the epic poem *The Song of Roland.* Name means "stag-bearer."

879. PAT—A 14.2-hand, 1,025 pound flea-bitten gray gelding, top rope horse in the 1940s and 1950s. He died in 1957 at age 22.

Paterson, A.B., poet—see REGRET (970).

Patton, George—see ALLAHMANDE, WITEZ II.

880. PATTY—Horse that, along with PET, pulled the Ingalls' family wagon to Oklahoma in the television show "Little House on the Prairie," which was based on the books by Laura Ingalls Wilder.

881. PAUL JONES—The 1920 Kentucky Derby winner, a brown gelding.

882. PEACOCK—Shakespearean actor Junius Brutus Booth's favorite pony. When the pony died, Booth wrapped him in white sheets and had a ceremony for him. Booth was the father of John Wilkes Booth, Lincoln's assassin, and of actor Edwin Booth.

883. PEANUTS—A 15.2-hand, 1,140-pound bay gelding, top rope horse in the 1940s and 1950s that was especially good with heavy cattle.

PEANUTS and PEANUTS II—see EXTERMINATOR.

Peck, Gregory—see LITTLE JOHN, MISTY (785).

884. PECOS—Wrangler Jane's horse in the television show "F Troop," 1965–1967.

Pecos Bill—see WIDOW-MAKER.

Pedersen, Lieutenant Eric—see RECKLESS.

885. PEDRO—The small burro mascot of *Boys' Life* magazine in the 1940s and 1950s. PEDRO was the mail-burro at the magazine.

886. PEGASUS—The great winged horse ridden by Bellerophon, the Prince of Corinth in Greek mythology. The name means "compact and strong" in Greek. Traditionally the horse is red because he sprang from the blood spilled when Perseus beheaded the Gorgon Medusa, his dam. He is also portrayed in Greek mythology as being a white winged stallion, created by Poseidon, god of the sea, in a contest with Athena to give the greatest gift to mankind. Athena won with the olive tree. PEGASUS was the special pet of Apollo and carried the thunder and lightning for him. He also carried thunderbolts for Zeus. Occasionally one of the nine Muses rode him around the sky. Bellerophon got a golden bridle from the gods to ride PEGASUS. Although Bellerophon did not tame PEGASUS, the horse willingly helped to kill the Chimera, after which Bellerophon tried to fly up to Olympus. PEGASUS bucked him off to earth and then returned to his pasture to be the pet of the Muses. Bellerophon's story is told in Nathaniel Hawthorne's *Wonder Book* and is also part of the story "The Chimera."

887. PEGASUS—Major Charles Emerson Winchester III's polo pony in the television show "M*A*S*H."

888. PEGASUS—The red flying-horse logo used by Mobil Oil Company. Also called the FLYING RED HORSE.

889. PELE—One of Eddie Macken's successful show jumpers.

Penfield, Colonel James—see BILLY (126).

Penn, William—see TAMERLANE.

890. PENSIVE—The 1944 Kentucky Derby winner, a chestnut colt.

THE PEOPLE'S HORSE—see CARRY BACK.

Pepe, movie—see DON JUAN (364), **KING COTTON**.

891. PEPPER—Johnny Nelson's horse in the Hopalong Cassidy stories. Johnny was Hopalong's sidekick.

Perrin, Jack—see STARLIGHT (1123).

Pershing, General John—see JEFF (592), KIDRON.

892. PERSIMMON—Won the English Derby in 1896 under the colors of Albert Edward, Prince of Wales.

Peschkof, Lieutenant Sotnik—see SERI.

893. PET—Along with PATTY, pulled the Ingalls' family wagon to Oklahoma in the television show "Little House on the Prairie," which was based on the books by Laura Ingalls Wilder.

PET—see DUCHESS.

894. PETER THE GREAT—The leading sire of Thoroughbred horses up to 1918.

895. PEYTONA—Chestnut mare that match-raced against FASHION in 1845 and won. Currier and Ives made a print of the race.

896. PHAETHON—One of the horses of Eos, the goddess of the dawn in classical mythology.

Phaeton—see AETHON (12), EOUS, PHLEGON, PYROIS.

897. PHANTOM—A racing pony in Marguerite Henry's book, *Misty of Chincoteague*.

898. PHANTOM—Zorro's white stallion in the television show, "Zorro," 1957–1959. Zorro's real identity was Don Diego de la Vega, and he was played by Guy Williams. Zorro's other horse was the black stallion TORNADO.

899. PHANTOM—A gray horse that performed diving acts in Atlantic City, New Jersey, in the 1950s. The horse dove off a 40-foot tower without a rider into a 12-foot deep tank of water.

"The Phantom," comic strip—see HERO (541), THUNDER (1181).

900. PHANTOM WINGS—One of the real MISTY's foals. MISTY's life was the basis for Marguerite Henry's book *Misty of Chincoteague*.

901. PHAR LAP—A great Australian racehorse that never got to compete in the United States because he died in California in 1932 at the age of 6 before his first American race. The death was said to have been caused by colic, but there were rumors of poisoning. He was stuffed and is in the National Museum of Victoria in Melbourne. His 14-pound heart is on display at the Australian Institute of Anatomy. The name means "lightning" in Singhalese, and his nicknames were THE

RED TERROR and THE KANGAROO HORSE. His story is told in the 1983 movie, *Phar Lap*.

902. PHARI—The pony in *Phari: Adventures of a Tibetan pony*.

903. PHIL SHERIDAN—One of Union Captain George A. Custer's horses during the Civil War, named after his cavalry commander.

Philip, Prince—see SAMSON.

Phillipa's Fox Hunt—see COCKATOO.

Phillips, John ("Portugee")—see UNKNOWN HORSE (1228).

Phillips, Stephen—see SLEEPY TOM.

904. PHLEGON—One of the bold white horses of Apollo/Helios, the sun god, that pulled the chariot across the sky in classical mythology. The glow of PHLEGON's breath reddens the western sky at the end of the day. His name means "raging fire." Once Apollo's half-human son, Phaeton, tried to drive the sun horses across the sky and failed.

905. PHOBOS—Ares'/Mars' horse in classical mythology. Name means "fear."

Pickens, Slim—see LITTLE JOHN.

Pickett, General George,—see LUCY.

906. PIE—James Stewart's favorite mount in his western movies. He first rode him in the 1950 movie, *Winchester '73* and for the last time in the 1968 movie, *Bandolero*.

907. THE PIE—The piebald horse ridden by Velvet Brown that wins the Grand National Steeplechase in Enid Bagnold's book, *National Velvet*. THE PIE is short for

THE PIEBALD. In the movie version, THE PIE is played by KING CHARLES, a grandson of MAN O' WAR, and was given to Elizabeth Taylor, who played Velvet, on her 14th birthday by the studio.

908. PIED PIPER—The wild pinto pony that sired Misty in real life and in Marguerite Henry's book, *Misty of Chincoteague.*

Piggott, Lester—see NEVER SAY DIE.

909. PINK—One of Union Captain Charles Hammond's war-horses in the Civil War, a Morgan of the Black Hawk strain. PINK died in 1886 at age 30, and his name is on a stone shaft in New York state commemorating the men of Company H and their horses.

910. PINK STAR—The 1907 Kentucky Derby winner, a bay colt.

Pirandello, Luigi, author—see FOFO.

911. PIRATE—A Shire horse painted by Zeitter in 1810.

912. PLAUDIT—The 1898 Kentucky Derby winner, a brown colt.

913. PLEASANT COLONY—The 1981 Kentucky Derby winner, a dark bay colt.

914. PLUTO—One of the foundation sires of the famous Lippizan horses of the Spanish Riding School.

915. PLUTO—The white Lippizan stallion that was imported from Austria to play the title role in the movie, *Florian.*

Pluto—see ABASTER, ABATOS, AETON, ALASTOR, NONIOS.

916. POCAHONTAS—A mare that held a world pacing record.

917. **POCO BUENO**—An American Quarter Horse that was a cutting-horse champion and a sire of good stock horses. His sire was KING.

918. **PODARGUS**—One of Hector's chariot horses in Homer's *Iliad*.

919. **POETHLYN**—The winner of the 1918 and 1919 Grand National Steeplechase.

920. **POKER CHIP PEAKE**—A dapple-gray gelding, top calf-roping horse in the 1950s and 1960s. He retired in 1965 after a trailer accident.

921. **POKEY**—Pee Wee Jenkins' horse in the television show "Fury" 1955–1966. Pee Wee was Joey Newton's friend.

922. **POKEY**—The pet pony owned by Gumby.

923. **POMPEIANUS**—Diocles' chariot racer in ancient Rome.

924. **PONDER**—The 1949 Kentucky Derby winner, a dark bay colt.

Ponset, Britt—see SCAR (1037).

Pony Bob—see UNKNOWN HORSES (1234).

A Pony Called Lightning—see LIGHTNING (678).

925. **POPCORN**—A 14.3-hand, 1,200-pound bay rope horse in the 1940s and 1950s. He died in 1955 at age 14 in a trailer accident.

PORCELLUS—see INCITATUS.

Portis, Charles, author—see BEAU, BO, JUDY, LITTLE BLACKIE.

Poseidon—see ARION, HIPPOCAMPUS, PEGASUS (886), STHENIUS.

Post, Wilber and Carol—see MR. ED (777).

Potter, Colonel Sherman—see SOPHIE.

Potts, Henry—see THE DUKE (383).

926. POWDER FACE—A horse used in a carnival diving act before 1924 for Dr. Carver, Sonora Carver's father-in-law. POWDER FACE dove without a rider from a 40-foot tower into an 11-foot tank of water. A later diving horse was named after this one.

927. POWDER FACE—A dapple-gray gelding that performed diving acts in Atlantic City, New Jersey, in the 1970s. The horse dove off a 40-foot tower with a rider into a 12-foot tank of water. Named after an earlier diving horse.

Power, Tyrone—see BARAKAT.

Powers, Tom—see RAJAH.

928. THE PRANCING HORSE—The emblem used by Enzo Ferrari on Ferrari cars.

Presley, Elvis—see SUN.

Preston, Sergeant William—see REX (974).

929. PRIDE—An Arabian horse that was a gift to Queen Elizabeth II from King Hussein of Jordan. PRIDE was a favorite mount of hers and was also ridden by young Princess Anne.

930. PRINCE—William F. ("Buffalo Bill") Cody's first horse, which he rode on a daring ride to warn his father of danger from proslavery advocates.

931. PRINCE CHARLIE—The large-boned bay horse ridden by Jack Jouett during the American Revolution. Jouett made a dangerous sixty-mile cross-country ride on PRINCE CHARLIE in order to warn Thomas Jefferson at Monticello that the British were coming. Also called PRINCE CHARLES. Called SALLIE in the children's book *Jack Jouett's Ride*, by Gail Haley.

932. PRINCE HAL—Pat Smythe's mount for the 1954 Grand Prix show jumping in Paris, France.

933. PRINCEQUILLO—A well-known Thoroughbred sire.

PRIVATE FIRST CLASS FEARLESS—see RECKLESS.

Prophet Strain—see MOHAMMED'S TEN HORSES.

934. PROUD CLARION—The 1967 Kentucky Derby winner, a bay colt.

Public Enemy, movie—see RAJAH.

935. PURGATORY—Dustin Farnum's horse in silent western movies.

PUROCIS—see PYROIS.

936. PURPLE STAR—Princess Anne's first horse.

937. PUTNAM—The army horse decorated by Pershing as the best artillery horse in the American Expeditionary Force in France during World War I.

Putnam, General Israel—see UNKNOWN HORSE (1229).

938. PYROIS—One of the wild white horses of the sun god Apollo/Helios that pulled the chariot across the sky in classical mythology. Name means "fiery heat." Also spelled PUROCIS. Apollo's half-human son, Phaeton,

once tried to drive the sun horses across the sky and failed.

Quantrill, William Clarke—see CHARLEY (255).

939. QUEENIE—One of the horses that pulled the Overland Stage in the 1939 movie, *Stagecoach*, starring John Wayne. Andy Devine drove the stage and shouted encouragement to the horses. There were three hitches of six horses each used on the stagecoach route.

940. QUEENIE—A trick horse in silent western movies.

941. QUICK DRAW MCGRAW—The cartoon horse in the 1959 television show, "The Quick Draw McGraw Show." QUICK DRAW MCGRAW was a marshal, and his voice was done by Daws Butler.

"The Quick Draw McGraw Show," television show— see BABA LOOEY, MARTHA, QUICK DRAW MCGRAW.

Quixote, Don—see CLAVILENO, ROSINANTE.

Rabelais, Francois, author—see GARGANTUA'S MARE.

942. RABICAN—Argalia's coal-black charger that eventually became the property of Rinaldo in Carolingian legend of medieval chivalry. RABICAN was a magic horse that fed on air. The name means "horse with dark tail and some white hairs."

943. RACER—Jondalar's young dark brown stallion in Jean Auel's novel about prehistoric times, *Plains of Passage*. Jondalar rode him with a halter and rope while Ayla rode WHINNEY without anything. They tamed horses in an age when most people still considered horses to be a food source. *Plains of Passage* is fourth in Auel's *Earth's Children* series.

Radio City Music Hall—see SISSY.

944. RAFTER—Richard Boone's horse's real name in the television show "Have Gun, Will Travel."

945. RAGTIME—The horse in Will James' book, *The Drifting Cowboy* that was the best bucking horse in the West.

946. RAIDER—Charles Starrett's white Arabian in early western movies.

947. RAIDER—The Durango Kid's horse in western movies.

948. RAJAH—The horse in the 1931 movie, *Public Enemy* that killed Samuel ("Nails") Nathan and then was killed by Tom Powers.

949. RAKSH—The golden-rose-colored dappled Arabian stallion with a black mane and tail, belonging to the Persian hero Rustum, or Rustem. Rustum's deeds are recorded in the Persian epic poem *Shah-Nama* or *The Book of Kings*. Also spelled RAKHSH, REKSH, and RUKSH. RAKSH would let no one but Rustum ride him and, he was true and intelligent. Both horse and man were killed by Rustum's jealous half-brother.

950. RAMBLING WILLIE—A pacer foaled in 1970 whose story is told in Donald P. Evans' book, *Rambling Willie, the Horse that God Loved.* The owners tithed the horse's winnings to their church, and the church members prayed when he was injured. As of 1981, RAMBLING WILLIE had earned $1,800,705.

Ramsey, Alec—see THE BLACK STALLION.

951. RANGER—An Arabian horse ridden by George Washington.

952. RANGER—The dapple-gray horse that U.S. Senator Glen Taylor from Idaho rode during his election campaign in 1942 because of the gasoline shortage.

953. RANGER—Roy Stewart's pinto in early western movies.

Rankin, Joe—see UNKNOWN HORSES (1238).

954. RAPID LAD—An English Thoroughbred that had a race named after him while he was still an active racehorse. He won his namesake race in 1987 but was placed second for interference; he finished third in 1988 in the race but was placed last for interference.

Rarey, John—see CRUISER.

Raspe, Rudolph Erich—see THE LITHUANIAN.

Raswan, Carl, author—see DRINKER OF THE WIND.

955. RATTLER—An American horse that raced against MISS TURNER, a Welsh mare, in the first international horse race in 1829 in England.

The Ravenswing—see EMPEROR.

956. RAWHIDE—Actor Jock Mahoney's buckskin stallion in the television show "The Range Rider."

957. RAZOR—Lucas McCain's (Chuck Connors) horse in the television show "The Rifleman."

Reagan, Nancy—see LITTLE BIT, NO STRINGS.

Reagan, President Ronald—see CATALINA, GUALI-ANKO, LITTLE MAN.

958. REBEL—Johnny Mack Brown's palomino horse in western movies.

959. RECKLESS—A small Korean racing mare that served as an ammunition carrier for a U.S. marine platoon during the Korean War. She was a 4-year-old, 14-hand mare with a blaze and three white socks purchased for

$250 in 1952. Her original name was AH-CHIM-HAI, which means "flame of the morning" in Korean. She was trained by Lieutenant Eric Pedersen and carried 75mm shells. One day she made 51 solitary runs for ammunition during the battle for Vegas, carrying six to ten rounds of ammunitions each trip. She received a medal for bravery under fire and was promoted to marine sergeant in 1954. RECKLESS later had a colt named PRIVATE FIRST CLASS FEARLESS.

960. RED—Billy the Kid's horse in the 1943 movie, *The Outlaw*. Billy the Kid's horse's name in real life in unknown.

961. RED A—One of David Broome's successful show jumpers.

962. RED BUCK—Outlaw Emmet Dalton's horse, ridden in a raid on Coffeyville in 1892.

963. RED EYE—Confederate General Richard Garnett's horse in the Civil War. Both were killed in the Battle of Gettysburg.

964. RED FOX—Outlaw Jesse James' favorite horse.

965. RED LIGHTNING—The racehorse that got shot during the seventh race by Nikki Arane in the 1956 movie, *The Killing*.

966. RED LIPS—The brown-and-white paint horse with blue eyes and a black tail that was part of a carnival diving act from about 1924 to 1932. The horse had been considered an outlaw but was easily trained to dive. Sonora Carver rode the horse off a 40-foot tower into an 11-foot tank of water. Sonora detached her retinas when she hit the water wrong in 1931 while riding RED LIPS. Sonora continued to ride in the act for 11 more years despite being blind. The act ended in 1942 due to the war.

The Red Pony, book—see GABILAN.

967. RED ROVER—The slower horse that was traded for LADY by Jess Birdwell in the movie, *The Friendly Persuasion,* based on the book by Jessamyn West.

968. RED RUM—A British steeplechaser, a bay gelding, that won the Grand National Steeplechase in 1977, ridden by Tommy Stack. RED RUM suffered from a bone disease similar to human arthritis but was still able to race. He won the Grand National Steeplechase three times.

THE RED TERROR—see PHAR LAP.

Redford, Robert—see RISING STAR.

969. REGRET—The 1915 Kentucky Derby winner, a chestnut filly. She was the first filly to win the Kentucky Derby, and she won wire to wire. She was undefeated after her Kentucky Derby win.

970. REGRET—The mare in A.B. Paterson's poem "The Man from Snowy River." It was the loss of REGRET's colt that made the man from Snowy River mount his hardy mountain horse and track the colt down in a wild-horse herd. The story is told in the 1983 movie *The Man from Snowy River.*

Reid, Dan—see VICTOR.

971. REIGH COUNT—The 1928 Kentucky Derby winner, a chestnut colt.

The Reivers, movie and book—see LIGHTNING (679).

REKSH—see RAKSH.

"The Restless Gun," television show—see SCAR.

972. REVELATION—A bay Standardbred horse with white markings, foaled in 1906, that became a successful fine-harness show horse, owned and shown by Loula Long. All of her horses had names ending with *-ion*. REVELATION died in 1935.

Revere, Paul—see SCHEHERAZADE, UNKNOWN HORSE (1225).

973. REX—The mean, almost unmanageable black Morgan stallion that starred in western movies in the 1920s and 1930s. He was known as the "King of the Wild Horses" and starred in the movies *Black Cyclone*, 1927; *The Law of the Wild*, 1934; and *The Adventures of Rex and Rinty*, 1935.

974. REX—Sergeant William Preston's horse in the 1955 television show "Sergeant Preston of the Yukon."

975. REX—Trick rider and roper Monte Montana's pinto horse. He named all his horses REX.

976. REX—American Saddlebred movie and television horse star in the late 1950s. He starred in the movies *The Fighting Stallion* and *Wide Country*, and in the 1965 television series "The Loner." MONTROSE SEA was REX's registered name.

977. REX BEACH—A tall Saddlebred horse that fended off a cougar that attacked his owner, Walter Devereaux, in Port Angeles, Washington, in 1931. He was nominated for a Latham Foundation Gold Medal for animal heroes.

978. REX DENMARK—A 15.2-hand, seal-brown American Saddle Horse stallion that was the sire of all the Rex line of saddlers, including REX MCDONALD. He was foaled in 1882 and was well mannered enough to be ridden by boys and women in shows during his five-year show career.

979. REX MCDONALD—A black American Saddle Horse stallion owned by Ben Middleton in the early 1900s. He was the "Dan Patch of the Saddle Horse World" and was called the "King of Saddle Horses." He was foaled in 1890 and died at the age of 23 in 1913. He is buried in the center field of the Mexico City Fairgrounds in Mexico, Missouri.

980. REX THE ROBBER—One of Alwin Schockemohle's successful show jumpers.

981. REYNOLDSTOWN—The winner of the 1935 and 1936 Grand National Steeplechase. He was the fifth to win the race twice and the third to win it in successive years.

Rhinestone Cowboy, record album—see JUNIOR.

982. RIBOT—A well-known Italian racehorse.

Richard I, (the Lion-hearted), King of England—see ALICE-OF-THE-NIGHT, FAUVEL, LYARD.

Richard II, King of England—see ROAN BARBARY.

Richard III, King of England—see WHITE SURREY.

983. RICHMOND—A bay stallion ridden by Confederate General Robert E. Lee during the beginning of the Civil War. The stallion was not suited for battle—he bit and kicked other horses and was too noisy. One story said that Lee got rid of the horse, a present from the citizens of Richmond, and another story said that the stallion died after a long march in the heat.

Ricketts, John Bill—see CORNPLANTER, JACK (578).

Riddle, Samuel—see MAN O' WAR, WAR ADMIRAL.

Ride a Wild Pony, movie—see TAFF.

Riders of the Pony Express—see SYLPH.

Riding High, movie—see BROADWAY JOE.

984. RIENZI—The tall, spirited, coal-black Morgan gelding with three white socks from the BLACK HAWK line of Morgans that was Union General Philip Sheridan's war-horse during the Civil War. He had been named after a Mississippi town and was well known for his great strength and beauty. He once galloped a total of 75 miles in one day as Sheridan raced back and forth on the road, rallying Union soldiers. He was never ill and was wounded only four times. He was called WINCHESTER by some after the battle at Winchester, but Sheridan and his men still called him RIENZI. RIENZI died in Chicago in his early 20s in 1878. He was stuffed and was placed in an exhibit at the Smithsonian Institution in Washington, D.C.

"The Rifleman," television show—see BLUE BOY, RAZOR.

985. RIGEL—One of the four Arabian stallions driven in a chariot race by Charlton Heston in the 1959 movie *Ben-Hur,* based on the book by Lew Wallace. All four horses were named after stars and were owned by the Sheik Ilderim. They were bright bays in the book and white in the movie.

986. RILEY—The 1890 Kentucky Derby winner, a bay colt.

Riley, Joe—see BUTTERMILK (214).

Rinaldo—see BAYARD (96), RABICAN.

987. RING EYE—One of Frog Millhouse's horses in movies.

988. RINGO—The real name of Steve McQueen's horse in the television show "Wanted—Dead or Alive."

989. RISING STAR—The chestnut Thoroughbred stallion star of the 1979 movie *The Electric Horseman,* with Robert Redford and Jane Fonda, based on the book by H.B. Gilmour. In the movie, Redford steals the valuable horse and plans to release him in the middle of wild-horse country. RISING STAR was played by a horse named LET'S MERGE.

RISING SUN— see SUN (1143).

Ritter, Tex—see WHITE FLASH.

990. RIVA RIDGE—The 1972 Kentucky Derby winner, a bay colt that also won the Belmont but not the Preakness.

991. ROAN ALLEN—An outstanding sire of Tennessee Walking Horses. His sire was BLACK ALLAN (ALLAN F-1) and his dam was GERTRUDE. Also referred to as ROAN ALLEN F-38.

992. ROAN BARBARY—The uneven-tempered horse that King Richard II loved like a son in William Shakespeare's play *King Richard II.*

993. ROANOKE—A black stallion ridden by Union General George A. Custer during the Civil War. ROANOKE was injured in battle.

994. ROARING RIVER—Racehorse whose blinkers came loose in a race. His jockey, Francisco Torres, leaned over and took them off the horse and put them in his mouth. ROARING RIVER finished first, his first win in 19 starts in 1987.

995. ROB ROY—BLACK BEAUTY's sire in Anna Sewell's book, *Black Beauty.*

Roberts, General Frederick—see VOLONEL.

Robertson, Dale—see HANNIBAL, LEO JR., OLD BLUE (846).

996. ROBIN—Mr. Neely's ice-wagon horse in the 1944 movie *Meet Me in St. Louis*.

ROBIN—see BOB.

Rochester, Edward—see MESROUR.

ROCINANTE—see ROSINANTE.

997. ROCKET—FLICKA'S crazy dam in Mary O'Hara's book *My Friend Flicka*.

998. ROCKY—Kermit ("Tex") Maynard's horse in western movies.

Roderick—see ORELIO.

Rodney, Caesar—see UNKNOWN HORSES (1237).

Rodrigo—see BABIECA.

999. ROEMER—An international champion Dutch Warmblood, brown with four white socks and a blaze.

Rogers, Roy—see TRIGGER, TRIGGER II.

Rogers, Will—see BOOTLEGGER, CHAPEL, COMANCHE (281), COWBOY, DOPEY, LETAN, SOAPSUDS, SUNDOWN, TEDDY.

1000. ROITELET—One of Napoleon Bonaparte's light-colored Arabian war stallions.

1001. ROLAND—The messenger horse in Robert Browning's poem "How They Brought the Good News from Ghent to Aix."

Roland—see VEILLANTIF.

1002. ROLLA—General Winfield Scott's 18-hand bay warhorse.

1003. RONALD—The 7th Earl of Cardigan's chestnut Thoroughbred war-horse in the Battle of Balaklava on October 25, 1854. The 1936 movie *The Charge of the Light Brigade* tells the story. RONALD's head was stuffed after his death. Cardigan sweaters were named after this earl.

Rookwood, book—see BLACK BESS (135).

Roosevelt, Archibald—see ALGONQUIN.

Roosevelt, Eleanor—see DOT.

Roosevelt, Ethel—see FIDELITY.

Roosevelt, President Franklin—see NEW DEAL.

Roosevelt, President Theodore—see BLEISTEIN, MANITOU.

Rooster Cogburn, movie—see BEAU.

The Roping Fool, movie—see DOPEY.

1004. ROSABELLA—One of Mary, Queen of Scots' horses.

1005. ROSINANTE—Don Quixote's sorry-looking stallion in Cervantes' book *Don Quixote*. Also spelled ROCINANTE or ROXINANTE. Rosin means "ordinary horse" and *ante* means "before," so the name means that the horse was ordinary before Don Quixote took him on his knight-errant missions.

Ross, Mattie—see LITTLE BLACKIE.

1006. ROSSIGNOL—One of Madame Chatelet's horses in the 1700s. Name means "nightingale."

Roughing It, book—see OAHU.

"The Rounders," television show—see OLD FOOLER.

1007. ROVING BOY—The horse that won the 1983 Alibhai Handicap at Santa Anita racetrack by a nose but then fell, breaking both hind legs, and had to be destroyed.

ROWDY—see NEGRITO.

Rowlandson, Thomas, artist—see GRIZZLE.

ROXINANTE—see ROSINANTE.

"The Roy Rogers Show," television show—see BUTTERMILK (213), TRIGGER, TRIGGER II.

1008. ROYAL GIFT—A gray Catalonian jack sire given to George Washington by King Charles III of Spain.

1009. ROYAL RU—A well-known American Saddle Horse.

1010. ROYAL STUDENT—The favorite in the 1953 Grand National Steeplechase. There was a collision between ROYAL STUDENT and KNOTHER, ridden by Mick Morrissey. ROYAL STUDENT lost his rider, and Morrisey was knocked into ROYAL STUDENT's saddle. They finished last.

1011. RUBE—A Belgian horse that starred in the movie, *Chester, Yesterday's Horse,* along with CHAMP, another Belgian horse.

1012. RUBIO—Winner of the Grand National Steeplechase in 1908. He was the first American-bred horse to win that race.

1013. RUE FEREE—A proven American Quarter Horse racehorse in the late 1960s.

1014. RUFFIAN—The 3-year-old filly that won the fillies' Triple Crown in 1975. She was in a match race with Kentucky Derby winner FOOLISH PLEASURE in 1975 and broke her ankle. She was put down and buried at New York's Belmont Park.

1015. RUGGED LARK—A bay champion American Quarter Horse stallion.

RUKSH—see RAKSH.

1016. RUSH—Al ("Lash") LaRue's black horse in western movies.

Russell, Charles—see MONTE (792).

Rustum—see RAKSH.

1017. RUSTY—A horse owned by Bob Steele.

1018. RUTH—Festus Haggen's mule in the television show "Gunsmoke," 1955–1975.

Ryan, Tom—see BLOSSOM.

Ryder, Red—see PAPOOSE, THUNDER.

Rysdyk, William—see HAMBLETONIAN.

RYSDYK'S HAMBLETONIAN—see HAMBLE-TONIAN.

1019. SAGR—The red desert stallion that races THE BLACK in the 1983 movie, *The Black Stallion Returns*.

1020. SAILOR—Spin's horse in the Spin and Marty segments on the television show, "The Mickey Mouse Club."

1021. ST. MAWR—A great stallion in D.H. Lawrence's novel, *St. Mawr*.

Saki (H.H. Munro), author—see THE BROGUE.

1022. SALLIE—The bay Thoroughbred mare ridden by Jack Jouett in the children's book *Jack Jouett's Ride*, by Gail Haley. He rode to warn the people of Virginia, including four signers of the Declaration of Independence, that the British were coming during the Revolutionary War in 1781. His horse in real life was called PRINCE CHARLIE.

1023. SALLIE GARDNER—One of four racehorses that were photographed in the 1870s to prove a bet that at one point while galloping, all four legs of a horse were off the ground. Leland Stanford bet correctly. Eadweard Muybridge was the photographer.

1024. SALOME—A black racing mare that Sam Hart won when he raced his mare BETSY against the devil in an old New England folktale. The horse eventually vanished, and Hart became a broken man.

1025. SALT PERDU—Villain Malcuidant's horse in the epic poem, *The Song of Roland*.

Salten, Felix, author—see FLORIAN.

1026. SALVADOR—A successful show jumper ridden by Harvey Smith.

1027. SAM—Union General William Tecumseh Sherman's 16.2-hand bay horse during the Civil War. Sherman made famous the saying "War is hell." SAM was a fast walker, and though he was wounded several times, he survived the Civil War and died in 1884.

1028. SAM—Horse ridden by 10-year-old Louis Abernathy for 2,500 miles to meet Colonel Teddy Roosevelt in 1910. It took Louis, and his brother Templeton and his horse GERONIMO, six weeks to ride from Oklahoma to New York to see Roosevelt.

1029. SAMMY—One of the Budweiser Clydesdale geldings from the eight-horse hitch that toured the fourteen western states.

1030. SAMSON—Prince Philip's horse in the Disney movie *Sleeping Beauty*.

1031. SAN DOMINGO—A mustang in Marguerite Henry's book *San Domingo* that was one of the Pony Express horses ridden by Peter Lundy.

1032. SAN QUININA—An elderly polo pony that lured Prince Charles back to riding when he took up polo at the age of 15.

1033. SANTA ANNA—A small horse ridden by Robert E. Lee in the Mexican War.

1034. SAQLAWIEH—One of the five gallant Arabian mares that passed the endurance test in Mecca in the 7th century and founded the most notable families of Arabians. All five are referred to as El-Khamsa ("the Five"), or Al Khamseh. SAQLAWIEH was white, and her name means "smooth one."

1035. SARDAR—A bay gelding given to Jacqueline Kennedy by the president of Pakistan during her visit to that country while John F. Kennedy was president of the United States.

Sass, Herbert Ravenel, author—see NORTHWIND.

Savage, Will—see DAN PATCH.

Savalas, Telly—see TELLY'S POP.

1036. SAVOY—The favorite horse of King Charles VIII of France named after the duke of Savoy, who gave him the coal-black horse. The horse was blind in one eye and very mean.

1037. SCAR—Britt Ponset's horse on the radio show "The Six-Shooter." Ponset was played by James Stewart.

1038. SCAR—Vint Bonner's horse in the television show "The Restless Gun," 1957–1960.

The Scarlet Empress, movie—see KING JOHN.

1039. SCHEHERAZADE—Paul Revere's mare in Robert Lawson's children's book *Mr. Revere and I.* Revere's horse's real name is in fact unknown.

Scheherazade—see THE EBONY HORSE.

Schilling, Louis—see TIPPERARY.

Schockemohle, Alwin—see REX THE ROBBER.

Scott, Robert—see SOCKS.

Scott, Sir Walter, poet—see BEVIS.

Scott, General Winfield—see NAPOLEON (805), ROLLA, WASHINGTON.

1040. SCOUT—The pinto horse ridden by Tonto, the Lone Ranger's sidekick, in the television show, "The Lone Ranger," 1949–1965. In early episodes the horse was called PAINT or WHITE FELLER.

1041. SCOUT—A white horse ridden by Jack Hoxie in his early silent western movies.

1042. SEA STAR—The orphaned Chincoteague pony in Marguerite Henry's book, *Sea Star, Orphan of Chincoteague* that was befriended by Paul and Maureen Beebe.

1043. SEABISCUIT—The well-known bay Thoroughbred racehorse that beat Triple Crown winner WAR ADMIRAL in a match race in 1938. A grandson of MAN

O'WAR, he was also known as THE BISCUIT and OLD IRON HORSE. His story is told in Ralph Moody's book, *Come On Seabiscuit*.

1044. SEATTLE SLEW—The 1977 Triple Crown winner, a dark bay. He was purchased by Washington logger Mickey Taylor in 1975 for $17,500. He was a clumsy yearling but was undefeated as a 2- and 3-year-old. He was the only Triple Crown winner to go into the races undefeated and was undefeated after that year. SEATTLE SLEW got sick and almost died in 1978, but he raced against the 1978 Triple Crown winner AFFIRMED in the Marlowe Cup that year and won. He was syndicated and retired to stud at the end of 1978, and his total winnings were $1,208,726.

1045. SECRETARIAT—The 1973 Triple Crown winner, a fiery red chestnut colt with a white blaze and three white socks, also known as SUPER RED. He was foaled March 30, 1970, at Meadow Farm, Virginia. He was the first Triple Crown winner since 1948. He won the Belmont portion of the Triple Crown by 31 lengths and was declared to be the Horse of the Century. His jockey for the Triple Crown was Ron Turcotte. Before he won the Triple Crown SECRETARIAT had been syndicated for $190,000 a share to 32 shareholders. He died October 4, 1989, when he had to be put down due to laminitis.

Seely, General Jack—see WARRIOR (1262).

1046. THE SEIAN HORSE—A large bay horse whose four owners all died. The name became an expression for a man cursed with bad luck.

1047. SENIK—One of the horses of the sun, along with ENIK, MENIK, and BENIK, in Persian mythology.

"Sergeant Preston of the Yukon," television show—see REX (974).

1048. SERI—Cossack officer Lieutenant Sotnik Peschkof's small light gray horse that he rode 5,400 miles in 1889. The journey took 191 days.

1049. SEVEN MINUTES TO MIDNIGHT—A well-known bucking rodeo horse whose name is a spin-off of the bucking horse MIDNIGHT.

Sewell, Anna, author—see BLACK BEAUTY (133), CAPTAIN (231), DUCHESS, GINGER, MERRYLEGS, ROB ROY.

1050. SHADOWFAX—Gandalf's white horse that could fly like the wind and let only Gandalf ride him in J.R.R. Tolkien's book *Lord of the Rings*.

Shaffer, Peter, playwright—see NUGGET.

1051. SHAFTER V—Jockey Bill Shoemaker's first winning mount, in 1949.

Shah-Nama—see RAKSH.

Shakespeare, William, author—see CAPILET, CURTAL, CUT, DOBBIN, GALATHE, ROAN BARBARY, UNKNOWN HORSES (1241), WHITE SURREY.

1052. SHAM—The pet name for THE GODOLPHIN BARB, given to the horse by Agba the stable boy in Marguerite Henry's book *King of the Wind*.

1053. SHANNON LASS—The mare that won the 1902 Grand National Steeplechase. She was the eleventh mare to win that race.

1054. SHARAD-NAR-AL-DIN—Mongolian conqueror Tamarlane's golden war-horse. Name means "my golden shadow." When his horse was killed underneath him in battle, Tamarlane vowed never to ride again.

1055. SHARATZ—The pinto war-horse stallion belonging to King Marko of the Empire of Serbia in the 14th century. The two were often described together as a dragon mounted on a dragon. The name means "piebald." King Marko died in 1399, and SHARATZ never allowed anyone else to ride him.

1056. SHARK—A descendant of MESSENGER.

Shatner, William—see TIME MACHINE, SULTAN'S GREAT DAY.

1057. SHEIK—Michael Ansara's horse's real name in the television show, "Broken Arrow."

The Sheik, movie—see ANNA.

Sheik Ilderim—see ALDEBARAN, ANTARES, ATAIR, RIGEL.

Sheldon, Ann, author—see CHICA D'ORO.

1058. SHENANDOAH—One of Union General Nathaniel Banks' war-horses in the Civil War.

1059. SHEPPERALK—A stallion in Lord Dunsay's *Book of Wonder.*

Sheridan, General Philip—see RIENZI.

1060. SHERMAN MORGAN—One of the three sons of JUSTIN MORGAN that helped to establish the Morgan breed.

Sherman, General William Tecumseh—see DOLLY (359), LEXINGTON (675), SAM (1027).

Sherwood, General Isaac—see FIREFLY (429).

1061. SHILOH—One of the legendary sires of the American Quarter Horse, foaled in 1844 in Illinois and imported to Texas in the late 1840s. He was half Thoroughbred with thick muscles and a heavy front end. He was to match-race 12-year-old STEEL DUST in 1855, but the race was canceled when STEEL DUST was injured in the chute.

1062. SHILOH—A sorrel mare that performed diving acts in Atlantic City, New Jersey, in the 1970s. The mare dove off a 40-foot tower with a rider into a 12-foot tank of water.

1063. THE SHIRKER—An honest 4-year-old racehorse in John Galsworthy's book, *Caravan: The Assembled Tales of John Galsworthy*. THE SHIRKER raced in the short story, "Had a Horse."

Shoemaker, Bill—see FERDINAND, GALLANT MAN, SHAFTER V.

1064. SHOTGUN—A small, sturdy saddle pony mare ridden by Albert Smith of Port Angeles, Washington, into a raging sea to pull a lifeboat full of stranded men to shore in 1930. She was nominated for the Latham Foundation Gold Medal for animal heroes in 1931.

SHURABAT AL-RIH—see DRINKER OF THE WIND.

1065. SHUT OUT—The 1942 Kentucky Derby winner, a chestnut colt.

Siegfried—see GRANI.

1066. SIGLAVY—One of the foundation sires of the Lippizan horses of the Spanish Riding School.

The Sign of Zorro, movie—see TORNADO.

Silas Marner, book—see WILDFIRE (1280).

1067. SILK STOCKINGS—A champion pacer whose story is told in the movie *Silky.*

1068. SILKY SULLIVAN—A well-known Thoroughbred racehorse.

SILVA—see CORNPLANTER.

1069. SILVER—The silver horse ridden by the Lone Ranger in the television show "The Lone Ranger," 1949–1965.

1070. SILVER—Sunset Carson's white horse in western movies.

1071. SILVER—Buck Jones' gray horse in early western movies. SILVER died in 1940 at about age 36.

1072. SILVER—A light sorrel gelding, top rope horse, ridden by Jake McClure in the 1920s and 1930s. McClure revolutionized the rodeo sport of calf roping. SILVER died in 1937 when he was hit by a car on the highway that went through the McClure ranch.

1073. SILVER BLAZE—The 5-year-old racehorse that was abducted and whose trainer was murdered in Sir Arthur Conan Doyle's short story "Silver Blaze," or "The Adventures of Silver Blaze." It turns out that it was the trainer who abducted the horse, and the horse that killed the trainer.

1074. SILVER BULLET—Whip Wilson's white horse in early western movies.

1075. SILVER CHIEF—One of the horses that played SILVER in the Lone Ranger movies.

1076. SILVER KING—One of the horses that played SILVER in the Lone Ranger movies.

1077. SILVER KING—Fred Thompson's dapple-gray Irish hunter in early western movies.

1078. SILVER KING—One of the carnival diving horses before 1924 that belonged to Dr. William Carver, Sonora Carver's father-in-law. SILVER KING dove, without a rider, off a 40-foot tower into an 11-foot tank of water.

SILVER TIP—see FUBUKI.

1079. SIMONA—One of Hartwig Steenken's successful show jumpers.

1080. SINGLE G—A successful pacer in the 1920s.

1081. SIR ARCHY—A racehorse that was the son of DIOMED. He match-raced against ECLIPSE (AMERICAN) in 1823 on the Union Race Course on Long Island and won. Forty thousand people watched the race.

1082. SIR BARTON—The 1919 Triple Crown winner, a bad-tempered chestnut colt. The first Triple Crown winner, he was also known as THE TENDER-TOED TYPHOON because he had tender feet and lost shoes easily.

1083. SIR GALLAHAD III—A Thoroughbred that sired three Kentucky Derby winners: GALLANT FOX, GALLAHADION, and HOOP JR.

Sir Gawain and the Green Knight, poem—see GRINGALET.

1084. SIR HUON—The 1906 Kentucky Derby winner, a bay colt.

1085. SIR PERICLES—The chestnut gelding, 14 hands and 7 years old, that was one of five horses given to Velvet

Brown by Mr. Cellini in Enid Bagnold's book, *National Velvet.*

1086. SISSY—A white Arabian mare used in the Christmas nativity scenes at Radio City Music Hall in the 1970s.

Sitting Bull, Chief—see BLACKIE (148), GRAY GHOST (513).

"The Six-Shooter," radio show—see SCAR (1037).

1087. SKINFAXI—Day god Dag's chariot horse in Nordic mythology. Name means "shining mane."

1088. SKIP—A plow horse used by Laura Ingalls Wilder after her marriage to Manly.

1089. SKOBELEF—The horse in Johan Bojer's *Skobelef Was a Horse.*

1090. SKOWRONEK—A well-known gray Arabian stallion foaled in 1909. He was imported to England from Poland and was owned by Lady Wentworth.

1091. SKYLARK—One of the horses ridden by Confederate General Jeb Stuart during the Civil War. He was a gift from a female admirer. SKYLARK once saved Stuart's life when he hurriedly mounted the horse without a bridle and jumped a fence in order to escape Union soldiers.

1092. SKYROCKET—Marty's horse in the Spin-and-Marty segments of "The Mickey Mouse Club" television show.

Sleeping Beauty, movie—see SAMSON.

1093. SLEEPY TOM—A blind pacer driven by Stephen Phillips.

1094. SLEIPNIR—The gray horse given to Odin, chief god in Norse mythology, by sly Loki. Said to be an eight-legged steed capable of traveling on land or sea. Name means "sly and slippery." SLEIPNIR is possibly the offspring of the old black stallion SVADILFARI, which was owned by a giant troll, and a pretty white mare sent to SVADILFARI to keep him from working on the wall of the gods at Asgard.

SLIM—see EXTERMINATOR.

Smith, Harvey—see SALVADOR.

Smith, Robyn—see NORTH SEA.

Smith, Tommy—see CANDY BOY, JAY TRUMP.

1095. SMOKEY—Lee Marvin's drunken horse in the 1965 movie *Cat Ballou.*

1096. SMOKY—The cow horse in Will James' book *Smoky, the Cowhorse,* gentled and started by the cowboy Clint. The movie role was played by a horse named COUNTRY GENTLEMAN.

Smythe, Pat—see FINALITY, FLANAGAN, PRINCE HAL.

1097. SNOW—A white mare used in a carnival diving act around 1924. Sonora Carver rode her off a 40-foot tower into an 11-foot tank of water. The mare was too greedy and ate herself out of a job when she got too fat to dive.

1098. SNOWBOUND—William Steinkraus's 10-year-old mount in the 1968 Olympics in Mexico City. They became the first Americans to win an individual jumping gold medal.

1099. SNOWFLAKE—Texas Guinan's white mare in western movies.

1100. SNOWFLAKE—Actor Wilford Brimley's gray speckled horse in television car commercials.

1101. SNOWMAN—A successful open jumper, a flea-bitten gray gelding, owned and trained by Harry de Leyer. He was a former plow horse, and Harry bought him for $80 from the knacker. At 12 years old he became a jumper, and at 16 he won the Madison Square Garden National Horse Show Horse of the Year award in 1958, then again in 1959.

1102. SNOWMANE—The white horse belonging to Theoden, king of the Golden Hall in J.R.R. Tolkien's book *Lord of the Rings.*

1103. SOAPSUDS—One of actor, roper, and entertainer Will Rogers' horses, a strawberry roan roping horse that Rogers rode in parades.

1104. SOCKS—The last of Arctic explorer Robert Scott's Siberian ponies to die in his 1910 expedition.

1105. SOLDIER BOY—One of William F. ("Buffalo Bill") Cody's horses from his scouting days. Mark Twain wrote about the horse in his short story, "A Horse's Tale."

1106. SOLIDO—A chestnut Peruvian Paso stallion featured in photographer Robert Vavra's 1989 book, *Vavra's Horses,* as one of the world's ten most beautiful equines.

1107. SOMBRA—An elderly polo pony that, along with SAN QUININA, helped lure Prince Charles back to riding when he took up polo at age 15.

Somerville, Edith, and Martin Ross, authors—see COCKATOO.

The Son of the Sheik, movie—see FIREFLY (430), JADAAN.

The Song of Roland, epic poem—see BARBAMOUCHE, GAIGNUN, MARMIORE, PASSECERF, SALT PERDU, SOREL, TACHEBRUN, TENCENDUR, VEILLANTIF.

1108. SOONER—A white Shetland pony that was, along with BOOMER, the mascot of the University of Oklahoma's football team, the Sooners, in the 1970s. The two ponies pulled a small covered wagon around the goalposts after touchdowns.

1109. SOPHIE—Colonel Sherman Potter's horse in the television show "M*A*S*H," 1972–1983.

1110. SOREL—Gerin's war-horse in the epic poem *The Song of Roland.*

SORREL—see OLD SORREL.

Southey, Robert, author—see NOBS, ORELIO.

1111. SPARK PLUG—A knock-kneed racehorse in the song and comic strip "Barney Google."

1112. SPECTACULAR BID—The 1979 Kentucky Derby winner, a dark bay colt, that came from behind to win by 2 ¾ lengths.

1113. SPEND A BUCK—The 1985 Kentucky Derby winner, a bay colt, whose time was one of the fastest Derbies ever won. The colt's owner decided against a Triple Crown attempt and raced the horse instead in the Jersey Derby. He won it and became the richest 3-year-old.

Spenser, Edmund, author—see BRIGADORE, SPU-MADOR.

Spin and Marty—see DYNAMITE, SAILOR, SKY-ROCKET.

1114. SPOKANE—The 1889 Kentucky Derby winner, a chestnut colt.

Sporting Blood, movie—see TOMMY.

1115. SPUMADOR—King Arthur's steed in Spenser's *Faerie Queene.* Name means "the foaming one."

1116. SPUNKY—Shirley Temple's horse in the 1935 movie, *Curly Top.* She got to keep the horse after the movie.

1117. SQUAW H—A Quarter Horse daughter of KING who was never beaten over a quarter-mile race.

Stack, Tommy—see RED RUM.

Stagecoach, movie—see BABY, BESSIE, BILL (122), BLACKIE (147), BONNIE, BRIDESMAID, CHILE, HONEY, QUEENIE (939), SWEETHEART.

Stanford, Leland—see SALLIE GARDNER.

Stanhope, Lady Hester—see LAILA, LULU.

Stanley, Dick—see STEAMBOAT (1124).

1118. STANLEYVILLE STEAMER—A zebra trained by Jim Papon to be a trotting horse.

STAR—see UNKNOWN HORSE (1239).

1119. STAR OF THE EAST—One of the horses ridden by Confederate General Jeb Stuart during the Civil War that broke down due to the long marches.

1120. STAR POINTER—A pacer that broke the harness racing 2-minute mile record in 1897 with a time of 1:59.25.

1121. STARLIGHT—Tim McCoy's white horse in western movies. Later he gave the horse to Bob Livingston to ride in western movies.

1122. STARLIGHT—One of Hoot Gibson's western movie horses in the 1930s.

1123. STARLIGHT—Jack Perrin's white horse in early western movies.

Starr, Belle—see VENUS.

Starrett, Charles—see RAIDER (946).

1124. STEAMBOAT—A dark horse with white socks that became America's first bucking horse. He was born in Wyoming before the turn of the century and was owned by John C. Coble. He started bucking at Wyoming's Frontier Days in 1901 and bucked for 13 years. Dick Stanley was the only rider ever to stay on long enough to make an official ride. He got his name because his breathing was noisy when he bucked due to broken nose bones that did not heal properly when he was a colt. Later he was called OLD STEAMBOAT. He is buried in Wyoming.

1125. STEAMBOAT—One of Daniel Webster's favorite horses. When the horse died, Webster buried him with halter and shoes on, standing upright in his grave.

1126. STEED—Dudley Do-Right's horse in the television cartoon show, "The Dudley Do-Right Show," 1969–1970.

1127. STEEL—A western movie horse in the 1940s, a chestnut stallion with a white blaze and flaxen mane and tail.

He was ridden by John Wayne in the movie *Conqueror,* by Robert Taylor in *Westward the Women,* and by Joel McCrea in *Buffalo Bill.* Randolph Scott also rode him in westerns.

1128. STEEL DUST—A foundation sire of the modern Quarter Horse, a bay that was foaled in 1843 and was a strain of the JANUS blood. He was foaled in Kentucky and brought to Texas in 1844. He was out of a Thoroughbred mare and he stood 15 hands and weighed 1,200 pounds. He was not a gray like his name suggests, for steel dust was a medical concoction of that time and was rusty in color; he was a bay. He was called the "fastest horse in the West" and sired good cow horses and racers.

Steele, Bob—see BANNER (85), BROWNIE, RUSTY.

Steenken, Hartwig—see KOSMOS, SIMONA.

Steinbeck, John, author—see GABILAN.

Steiner, Stan, author—see WHITE STAR.

Steinkraus, William—see SNOWBOUND.

1129. STELLA MOORE—A champion Quarter Horse that lost a match race against Thoroughbred OLYMPIA over almost a quarter-mile track in 1949.

Stevens, Gary—see WINNING COLORS.

1130. STEVENSON MARE—The mare that was bred with DENMARK in 1851 to start the American Saddlehorse breed.

Stewart, James—see PIE (906), SCAR (1037).

Stewart, Captain James—see TARTAR (1166).

Stewart, Roy—see RANGER (953).

1131. STHENIUS—One of Poseidon's horses in classical mythology.

1132. STONE STREET—The 1908 Kentucky Derby winner, a bay colt.

1133. STORMY—Gordon ("Wild Bill") Elliot's horse in western movies.

1134. STORMY—MISTY's foal in Marguerite Henry's book *Stormy, Misty's Foal* based on the real Chincoteague pony MISTY's life. STORMY was owned by Paul and Maureen Beebe.

"Straight Arrow," radio show—see FURY (467).

1135. STRAWBERRY—A tired old cab horse in C.S. Lewis's fantasy series *The Chronicles of Narnia*.

"Strawberry Roan," movie—see TARZAN.

1136. STREIFF—The favorite war-horse of King Gustavus Adolphus of Sweden. Name means "raider."

1137. STRIDER—A piebald horse in Leo Tolstoy's story, *Strider: the Story of a Horse*.

1138. STROLLER—A show-jumping pony ridden by Marion Coakes in the late 1960s. The 14.2-hand bay pony was also ridden in the Mexico City Olympic Games for Great Britain.

Stuart, James Ewell Brown (Jeb)—see BULLET, CHANCELLOR, GENERAL (483), HIGH SKY, LADY MARGRAVE, MARYLAND, SKYLARK, STAR OF THE EAST, VIRGINIA.

Stuckelberger, Christine—see GRANAT.

1139. STYMIE—A high-headed chestnut racehorse that was a public favorite.

Suez, movie—see BARAKAT.

1140. SULTAN—A Thoroughbred presented to Queen Elizabeth II by the president of Pakistan in 1959.

1141. SULTAN'S GREAT DAY—A black American Saddlebred stallion owned by William Shatner in the late 1980s. He was a breeding stallion and a former two-time Fine Harness Horse World Champion. He was featured in photographer Robert Vavra's 1989 book, *Vavra's Horses,* as one of the world's ten most beautiful equines.

1142. SUMMERTIME PROMISE—A racehorse that was fitted with size-B foam brassiere inserts on her rear ankles in order to cushion her pounding legs.

1143. SUN—A palomino horse owned by Elvis Presley in the 1960s. Also called RISING SUN.

1144. SUNDAY SILENCE—The 1989 Kentucky Derby winner, a colt who ran the slowest Derby in 31 years. It was also the coldest Derby in 72 years, only 44°. SUNDAY SILENCE almost died twice before getting to the Kentucky Derby, and he swerved left and right down the stretch drive as his jockey whipped him.

1145. SUNDOWN—One of roper, actor, and entertainer Will Rogers' polo horses, a dapple gray.

1146. SUNNY—Vice President Walter Mondale's daughter Eleanor's Quarter Horse, a palomino show horse.

1147. SUNNY JIM—A small bay movie specialty horse used for transfers, in which his rider would leap off of him onto a train at a gallop.

1148. SUNNY'S HALO—The 1983 Kentucky Derby winner, a chestnut colt with a white blaze, and one of the few Kentucky Derby winners not foaled in the United States.

1149. SUNSET—Jimmy Wakely's palomino horse in western movies.

SUPER RED—see SECRETARIAT.

Supergirl—see COMET (282).

Surtees, Robert S., author—see ARTERXERXES, XERXES.

1150. SVADILFARI—An old black stallion in Norse mythology that hauled stones the size of mountains to help a giant troll build the wall of the gods in exchange for the sun and the moon and the goddess Freya. Name means "slippery place." Possibly the sire of SLEIPNIR.

1151. SWALE—The 1984 Kentucky Derby winner, a dark bay colt.

1152. SWAPS—The 1955 Kentucky Derby winner, a chestnut colt. He died in 1972.

Swayze, Patrick—see BR FEROUK ROBERT.

1153. SWEETHEART—The name of one of the horses that pulled the Overland Stage in the 1939 movie *Stagecoach,* starring John Wayne. Andy Devine drove the stage and shouted encouragement to the horses. There were three hitches of six horses each used on the stagecoach route.

Swift, Jonathan, author—see HOUYHNHNMS.

1154. SYLPH—The bay Thoroughbred mare ridden on the first leg of the first Pony Express relay westward by

Johnny Frey in Ralph Moody's book, *Riders of the Pony Express*.

1155. SYLVAAN—SILVER's sire in the Lone Ranger comic books.

1156. SYLVESTER—Professor Marvel's horse in the 1939 movie, *The Wizard of Oz*.

1157. SYLVESTER—The gray jumping horse from the 1985 movie, *Sylvester*. SYLVESTER was trained and ridden by Melissa Gilbert in the movie.

1158. T.D.—A miniature stallion standing 28¾ inches tall that was the mascot for the Denver Broncos in the 1970s.

1159. TACHEBRUN—Ganelon's war-horse in the epic poem *The Song of Roland*. Name means "brown spot."

1160. TAFF—The white pony in the 1976 Disney movie *Ride a Wild Pony*.

"Tales of Wells Fargo," television show—see LEO JR.

1161. TALL BULL—One of the fast horses that William F. ("Buffalo Bill") Cody rode during his scouting and Indian-killing days. Named by Cody after the Cheyenne war chief Tall Bull, who died in the battle in which the horse was captured. The big bay had belonged to Tall Bull, whom many think Cody killed. Others think Cody was given the chief's horse. Cody often rode the horse bareback.

Tamarlane—see SHARAD-NAR-AL-DIN.

1162. TAMERLANE—A stallion imported to America by William Penn in 1699.

1163. TANGO DUKE—The oldest racehorse on record, a bay gelding foaled in 1935 who died in 1978 at 42 years of age.

1164. TARGET—One of Annie Oakley's horses in the television show "Annie Oakley."

1165. TARTAR—The spirited Arabian ridden by Jefferson Davis during the Mexican War.

1166. TARTAR—One of Union Captain James Stewart's war-horses during the Civil War. TARTAR had been abandoned when he got distemper, but was found again later. He was wounded by shells which shot off his tail and was again left behind, but he jumped a fence in order to rejoin the troop.

1167. TARTAR—A small dark brown horse ridden by Queen Victoria.

1168. TARZAN—The palomino movie horse ridden by Ken Maynard in western movies in the 1930s. Maynard rode with Hoot Gibson and Bob Steele. Ken was a singing cowboy, and TARZAN was intelligent and knew many tricks. TARZAN starred in the 1933 movie *Strawberry Roan*. Maynard named him TARZAN after the character in his friend Edgar Rice Burroughs' books.

1169. TAURIS—One of Napoleon Bonaparte's light-colored Arabian war-horses, a silvery grey Persian mare with a white mane, given to him by Czar Alexander of Russia. TAURIS was excitable and high spirited.

Taylor, Elizabeth—see BEAUTY (102), THE PIE (907).

Taylor, Senator Glen—see RANGER (952).

Taylor, Mickey—see SEATTLE SLEW.

Taylor, Robert—see STEEL.

Taylor, General Zachary—see OLD WHITEY.

1170. TEABISCUIT—The winning racehorse in the 1943 Abbott and Costello movie *It Ain't Hay.*

1171. TEAM SPIRIT—The American horse that won the Grand National Steeplechase in 1964, the first American horse to do so in 26 years.

1172. TEDDY—One of roper, actor, and entertainer Will Rogers' horses, a dark bay that he named after Theodore Roosevelt. Rogers would rope the horse as the horse ran across the stage in their act. TEDDY wore special boots so he would not slip.

1173. TELLY'S POP—Telly Savalas's racehorse.

Temple, Shirley—see SPUNKY.

1174. TEN BROECK—Raced in 1877 at Pimlico against TOM OCHILTREE and PAROLE. PAROLE won. The U.S. Congress adjourned for this race, and Currier and Ives made a print of it.

1175. TENCENDUR—King Charlemagne's war-horse in the epic poem *The Song of Roland.* Name means "strife."

THE TENDER-TOED TYPHOON—see SIR BARTON.

1176. TERRANG—A well-known Thoroughbred racehorse.

1177. TETRARCH—A spotted English racehorse considered the fastest horse of all times. He had to retire early due to leg injuries caused by his hind hooves cutting up his forelegs.

1178. TEX—The pet pony given to Caroline and John Kennedy, Jr., by Vice President Lyndon Johnson.

Tex, book and movie—see NEGRITO.

"The Texan," television show—see DOMINO (360).

Thackeray, William Makepeace, author—see EM-PEROR.

THANKFUL'S MAJOR—see NEVELE PRIDE.

Theoden—see SNOWMANE.

Thomas, General George—see BILLY (124).

Thompson, Captain Earl F.—see JENNY CAMP.

Thompson, Fred—see SILVER KING (1077).

Thornton, Alicia—see LOUISA, ZINGARILLO.

1179. THREE BARS—A Thoroughbred sire of the modern Quarter Horse racehorse. He was bought for $300 and was later given away.

The Three Musketeers—see D'ARTAGNAN'S HORSE.

Three Stooges—see NELLIE (817).

1180. THUNDER—Red Ryder's black horse on radio, early western movies, and cartoons.

1181. THUNDER—Phantom's first horse in "The Phantom" comic strip.

1182. THUNDERBOLT—Johnny West's toy horse.

1183. THUNDERHEAD—The albino offspring of the mare FLICKA in Mary O'Hara's book *Thunderhead.*

Thunderhead, book—see BANNER (84), FLICKA, THUNDERHEAD.

1184. THUNDERHOOF—The black-and-white wild stallion star of the 1948 movie *Thunderhoof.*

Tilghman, Deputy Sheriff Bill—see CHANT.

Tilghman, Colonel Tench—see UNKNOWN HORSE (1231).

1185. TIM TAM—The 1958 Kentucky Derby winner, a dark bay colt. He raced in the Belmont but broke a bone in his foot and never raced again.

1186. TIME MACHINE—William Shatner's favorite American Saddle Horse in the late 1980s.

1187. TIPPERARY—A well-known bay gelding bucking rodeo horse, born in 1910 and died in 1932, in South Dakota. He was lost for a while and was thought, during that time, to be the trusted pet of 12-year-old Louis Schilling, a blind boy.

1188. TIPPERARY TIM—An Irish horse that won the 1928 Grand National Steeplechase at 100 to 1 odds. He and BILLY BARTON were the only two horses to finish out of 42 starters.

Toad, J. Thaddeus—see CYRIL.

Todd, Mark—see CHARISMA.

Tolkien, J.R.R., author—see SHADOWFAX, SNOW-MANE.

Tolstoy, Leo, author—see FROU FROU, STRIDER.

1189. TOM FOOL—A bay Thoroughbred racehorse.

1190. TOM HAL—A blue roan Canadian pacer, foaled in 1806, that contributed to the development of the American Saddle Horse breed. He was imported to Philadelphia from Canada. He died in 1847 at age 41.

1191. TOM OCHILTREE—Raced in 1877 at Pimlico against TEN BROECK and PAROLE. PAROLE won. The U.S. Congress adjourned in order to attend this race, and Currier and Ives made a print of it.

1192. TOM THE POLO PONY—A pony that is overfed by his master in Hilaire Belloc's book *New Cautionary Tales for Children*.

1193. TOMBOY—Stuart Hamblen's horse in movies.

1194. TOMMY—The fictional winner of the Kentucky Derby in the 1931 movie, *Sporting Blood*.

1195. TOMY LEE—The 1959 Kentucky Derby winner, a bay colt, one of the few Kentucky Derby winners not foaled in the United States.

Tonto—see SCOUT (1040).

1196. TONY—The sorrel with white stockings and blazed face that was owned and ridden by Tom Mix, an early western movie star. TONY starred in many movies, including the 1922 movie, *Just Tony*, which was based on a story by Max Brand. TONY was often called TONY THE WONDER HORSE. Tom and Tony did not use doubles in their movies. Both their footprints are in the sidewalk outside Grauman's Chinese Theater in Hollywood. Tom rode a younger horse, TONY JR., after TONY retired. Tom Mix died in a car accident in 1940, and TONY died at age 34 in 1944.

1197. TONY JR.—One of the horses that played Gene Autry's horse CHAMPION in the television show

"The Adventures of Champion." He had been ridden by Tom Mix after the original TONY retired.

TONY THE WONDER HORSE—see TONY.

1198. TOP GALLANT—An early trotting horse that won the first trotting race on a regulation track in America.

1199. TOPPER—William ("Hopalong Cassidy") Boyd's white horse in the 1948 television show "Hopalong Cassidy." TOPPER also starred in Cassidy's early western movies.

1200. TORNADO—Zorro's black stallion in the television show "Zorro," 1957–1959, and the 1960 movie *The Sign of Zorro*. Zorro's true identity was Don Diego de la Vega, played by Guy Williams. Zorro also had a white stallion named PHANTOM. TORNADO in the television show was played by a black Morgan gelding whose real name was DIAMOND DECORA-TOR. He had previously been shown in stock-horse competitions.

Torres, Francisco—see ROARING RIVER.

1201. TOSSY—The circus pony that Jackie Gleason bought for his daughter in the 1963 movie *Papa's Delicate Condition*. In order to buy the pony, Gleason had to buy the whole circus.

The Tour of Doctor Syntax in Search of the Picturesque, artistic plates—see GRIZZLE.

1202. TRAVELER I—The first of the white mascot horses for the University of Southern California football team, the Trojans.

1203. TRAVELLER—The favorite iron-gray Saddlebred war-horse of Confederate General Robert E. Lee. The spirited gelding had a black mane and tail and was purchased by Lee in the mid-1800s for $200. He had been named JEFF DAVIS and GREENBRIER before Lee renamed him TRAVELLER. Lee rode him during the Civil War and was very devoted to the horse even though other people said that the horse was difficult to ride. TRAVELLER marched in Lee's funeral procession in 1870 and died one or two years later from an infected nail-puncture wound. He was buried on the campus of Washington and Lee University in Virginia, but later his bones were unearthed and put on exhibit at the museum on the campus.

1204. TRAVELLER—One of Winston Churchill's horses, which he rode in point-to-point races.

The Travels of Baron Munchausen—see THE LITHU-ANIAN.

1205. TRICKSY—The Shetland pony that Natalie Clifford Barney, an American millionairess who lived in Paris, had as a child. Writers and intellectuals visited Barney often in Paris. Barney died in 1972.

1206. TRIGGER—The golden palomino horse with white mane, tail, and stockings that was ridden by Roy Rogers in 87 western movies and in "The Roy Rogers Show" on television for 6 ½ years. Roy had not ridden much when he bought TRIGGER and made his first movie in 1937. TRIGGER knew 50 tricks, was housebroken for tours, and often stole the show from Roy. Star of the 1946 movie *My Pal Trigger,* he was said to be the "smartest horse in the movies." His hoofprints are in front of Grauman's Chinese Theater in Hollywood. TRIGGER lived into his early 30s and died on July 3, 1965. He is now stuffed and displayed in the Roy Rogers–Dale Evans Museum in Victorville, California.

1207. TRIGGER II—TRIGGER's replacement in "The Roy Rogers Show." TRIGGER II is also mounted at the Roy Rogers–Dale Evans Museum.

1208. TRIXY—Laura Ingalls Wilder's saddle horse after her marriage to Manly.

Troilus and Cressida, play—see GALATHE.

1209. THE TROJAN HORSE—The legendary wooden horse made by the ancient Greeks and used as a way to get inside the walled city of Troy. The horse was made to hold 25 armed soldiers inside, and once they were within the walls, they were able to defeat the Trojans during the Trojan War. Inspired by the goddess Athena, they made the horse a brown mare with jewels for her eyes, mane, and tail. Odysseus was one of the 25 soldiers inside the horse. The story is told in Homer's *Iliad.*

1210. THE TROJAN HORSE—The white mascot horse of the University of Southern California Trojans football team. The mascot was TRAVELER I in the 1960s, TRAVELER II in the 1960s and 1970s, and TRAVELER III in the 1970s.

1211. TROTTER—An army mule mascot that was the last serial-numbered army mule.

1212. TRUE BRITON—A racing stallion and former warhorse of a British officer that is thought to be the sire of Justin Morgan. He was also called BEAUTIFUL BAY.

True Grit, book and movie—see BEAU, BO, JUDY, LITTLE BLACKIE.

1213. TRUXTON—Racehorse purchased by Andrew Jackson to race against GREYHOUND in order to pay off Jackson's debts. TRUXTON won, and Jackson went on to become president.

Tschiffely, Aime F.—see GATO, MANCHA.

"Tumbleweeds," comic strip—see BLOSSOM.

1214. TUNIS—The big black gelding that the French general Georges Boulanger rode after being appointed minister of war.

Turcotte, Ron—see FLAG OF LEYTE GULF, SECRETARIAT.

Turpin, Dick—see BLACK BESS (135).

Twain, Mark—see JERICHO, OAHU, SOLDIER BOY.

Twelfth Night, play—see CAPILET.

1215. TWENTY GRAND—The 1931 Kentucky Derby winner, a bay colt.

1216. TWILIGHT TEAR—A successful racehorse filly.

1217. TWINKLE—A colt in Lawrence Barrett's book *Twinkle, a Baby colt.*

Tyler, President John—see THE GENERAL (484).

Tyler, Tom—see ACE (10), BARON (91).

1218. TYPECAST—A Thoroughbred mare sold at auction for a record-breaking $725,000 in 1973.

1219. TYPHOON II—The 1897 Kentucky Derby winner, a chestnut colt.

Tziminchac—see EL MORZILLO.

1220. U.V.M. PROMISE—A Morgan show stallion in the 1970s.

1221. UBAYYAH—One of the five gallant Arabian mares that passed the endurance test in Mecca in the 7th century and founded the most notable families of Arabian horses. All five are referred to as El-Khamsa ("the Five"), or Al Khamseh. UBAYYAH was a dappled gray, and her name means "fortunate one."

1222. UCCAIHSRAVAS—The horse that was produced from the ocean by Kurma in Vedic mythology.

1223. UNBRIDLED—The 1990 Kentucky Derby and Breeders' Cup Classic winner, a bay colt with a white blaze, owned by 92-year-old Frances Genter.

1224. UNE DE MAI—A French trotting mare that raced against NEVELE PRIDE and won the International Trot.

Union Pacific—see BLIND TOM.

United States Congress—see PAROLE, TEN BROECK, TOM OCHILTREE.

University of Oklahoma Sooners—see BOOMER, SOONER.

University of Southern California Trojans—see TRAVELER I, THE TROJAN HORSE (1210).

University of Wyoming Cowboys—see COWBOY JOE.

1225. UNKNOWN HORSE—The name of the horse Paul Revere rode on his historic midnight ride, April 18, 1775, has never been known, according to most scholars. It is known only that it was a light and surefooted chestnut Narragansett pacer mare, of small size and good quality, borrowed from Deacon John Larkin's stable. Some say, however, that her name was BROWN BEAUTY. After his ride, which was done at a walk and trot mostly, Revere warned Adams and Hancock in Lexington that the British were coming. Revere and the mare were later captured by the British and the mare was kept. Dr. Prescott continued on to warn Concord after Revere was captured. Revere, one of the Sons of Liberty, usually rode his own horse, a gray mare, on his minuteman missions.

1226. UNKNOWN HORSES—Joan of Arc had four horses whose names were unknown. One was a black draft-type stallion, and one was white.

1227. UNKNOWN HORSE—A small black mare saved the life of Dr. Ephraim McDowell in a snowstorm. He was the first doctor to perform surgery on the abdomen.

1228. UNKNOWN HORSE—A 17-hand, 1,200-pound white Thoroughbred stallion was ridden from Fort Kearny, Wyoming Territory, in 1866 through freezing weather to Laramie, Wyoming, 236 miles away, to get help to stave off an Indian attack. The horse died after the four-day ride to Laramie but is credited with saving over 100 lives. His rider was John ("Portugee") Phillips, who borrowed the horse from an officer. The State of Wyoming has erected a marker where the gallant horse dropped, but never paid Phillips any money for the ride, though Phillips' widow was given some money by Congress after his death. In 1868, after a new treaty gave the Indians land which included Fort Kearny, the Indians burned the fort to the ground.

1229. UNKNOWN HORSE—General Israel Putnam's white horse in the Battle of Bunker Hill in 1775. During battle, Putnam told his troops, "Don't fire until you see the whites of their eyes." Later, in 1779, Putnam distracted the British so that his men could seek safety. When the British charged, he rode his white horse recklessly down a very steep hill and was safe from capture. That event is now known as "Putnam's Leap."

1230. UNKNOWN HORSE—Emily Geiger rode her unknown horse through British lines on her way to

Sumter to deliver a message from Greene during the American Revolution. She was stopped by the British, but they allowed her to go on.

1231. UNKNOWN HORSE—Colonel Tench Tilghman rode his unknown horse on a four-day journey spreading the news that Lord Cornwallis had surrendered in the American Revolution. His final destination was the Continental Congress at Philadelphia.

1232. UNKNOWN HORSE—During the Battle of the Alamo in 1836, Colonel Travis sent a courier from the Alamo to Goliad, 150 miles away, to ask for reinforcements. The courier, dressed as a Mexican woman, rode an unknown horse. The horse fell several times, but endured until they reached Goliad. The reinforcements never got to the Alamo, and all the defenders died.

1233. UNKNOWN HORSES—Lieutenant Archibald Gillespie and his men were sent to the West to find Captain Fremont so that California could be obtained for the United States in the mid-1800s. Gillespie's men rode exhausted and unknown horses through Indian country to find Fremont.

1234. UNKNOWN HORSES—The Pony Express lasted for eighteen months in 1860 and 1861. Five hundred unknown horses were used for this dangerous route from Sacramento, California, to St. Joseph, Missouri. Many were half-wild California mustangs, stallions, and mares. They generally bucked and reared before settling into their run. Robert ("Pony Bob") Haslam was one of the Pony Express riders. He made one ride of 380 miles in 36 hours, and in 1861 helped to carry President Lincoln's inaugural address, riding 120 miles in 8 hours, 10 minutes, using thirteen different ponies.

1235. UNKNOWN HORSE—Lieutenant Colonel George A. Custer's Crow scout Curley was told to dress like a

Sioux and escape with the Indians and then ride to General Terry to tell him of the battle going on with Custer and the 7th Cavalry. Curley escaped on an unknown horse, but there was no help for Custer and his men.

1236. UNKNOWN HORSES—Dr. Marcus Whitman and a companion rode unknown Appaloosa horses (15.2 to 16 hands, and dark purplish-blue with white spots on their hips) 3,500 miles to Washington, D.C., from Oregon in 1842 in order to convince Congress not to let any other country claim Oregon. Their trip was long and arduous but successful. In 1846 Congress adjusted the boundaries between the United States and Canada to the 49th parallel so that Oregon was saved for the U.S. Later Indians massacred Dr. Whitman and his family because of the measles epidemic that the settlers had brought.

1237. UNKNOWN HORSES—Caesar Rodney rode four unknown horses 86 miles in order to cast his vote for the colony of Delaware on the question of independence from Great Britain in 1776. He rode a trusty chestnut gelding, 14 hands, descended from the Virginia stallion JANUS; a bay filly that was a cross between an English mare and a Spanish pony; a sorrel Narragansett pacer mare; and finally, a fine, long-legged dapple-gray Thoroughbred. He arrived tired, scratched, and dirty but in time to vote and later to sign the Declaration of Independence.

1238. UNKNOWN HORSES—Scout Joe Rankin rode 160 miles in 28 hours from Milk Creek, Colorado, to Rawlins, Wyoming, to get help for U.S. Army troops trapped by Indians in 1879. He rode four unknown horses—a black part Thoroughbred, a brown-and-white pinto, a roan stallion, and a mustang. He got help, and the siege was broken.

1239. UNKNOWN HORSE—Sybil Ludington rode a young horse through 50 miles of wilderness to warn people that the British were coming. Her horse's name is unknown, but it is called STAR in Erick Berry's children's book about the ride.

1240. UNKNOWN HORSE—John Wilkes Booth escaped on horseback after shooting President Abraham Lincoln in 1865. The mare's name is unknown; she was described as a small but fast young roan.

1241. UNKNOWN HORSES—A jennet and a stallion are described but not named in William Shakespeare's poem *Venus and Adonis*.

1242. UPSET—The only horse ever to win against MAN O'WAR, in the Sanford Memorial Stakes in 1919 by half a length.

1243. VAGRANT—The 1876 Kentucky Derby winner, a brown gelding.

Valentino, Rudolph—see ANNA, FIREFLY (430), JADAAN.

1244. VALKYRIE—A pony ridden by Prince Andrew as a boy.

Valley of the Horses, book—see WHINNEY.

Van Dusen, Clyde—see CLYDE VAN DUSEN.

Vavra's Horses, book—see DEJADO, EL CORDOBES, EXCELADDINN, FLAMING TRON KU, GAI PARADA, GOLD DOUBLOON, LEOPARDO III, LORD APPLETON, SOLIDO, SULTAN'S GREAT DAY.

1245. VEILLANTIF—The horse belonging to the medieval French knight Roland, nephew of Charlemagne, in the epic poem, *The Song of Roland*. The name means "wide awake."

1246. VENETIAN WAY—The 1960 Kentucky Derby winner, a chestnut colt. His jockey, Bill Hartack, has ridden five Kentucky Derby winners.

Venezia, Mike—see DRUMS IN THE NIGHT.

1247. VENUS—The spirited black mare belonging to Belle Starr, the "Bandit Queen" rustler in Oklahoma.

Venus and Adonis, poem—see UNKNOWN HORSES (1241).

1248. VERMONT BLACK HAWK—A grandson of Justin Morgan that was part of the early family of BLACK HAWK Morgans.

1249. VIC—Lieutenant Colonel George A. Custer's young Kentucky Thoroughbred sorrel horse, killed in the Battle of Little Big Horn in 1876. Some sources say that VIC may have survived the battle, as a similar-looking horse was later seen.

1250. VICTOR—The horse belonging to Dan Reid, the Lone Ranger's nephew, in the television show "The Lone Ranger," 1949–1965.

Victoria, Queen of England—see FYVIE, LEOPOLD, LOCHNAGAR, MONARCH, TARTAR (1167).

1251. VINGSKORNIR—Brunhild's horse in Nordic legend.

1252. VIRGINIA—A big-boned bay Thoroughbred mare with black points and a white star that was ridden by Confederate General Jeb Stuart during the Civil War.

He rode her at the Battle of Gettysburg. She contracted distemper shortly after that and died.

The Virginian, book—see MONTE (793).

Vishnu—see KALKIN.

1253. VIZIR—One of Napoleon Bonaparte's favorite gray Arabian war stallions.

1254. VOLONEL—British General Frederick Roberts' white war charger in 1880 in the Afgan campaign.

1255. VOLUPTUARY—The 1884 winner of the Grand National Steeplechase. He retired to the stage at the Drury Lane Theatre, where he jumped a water jump in the play, *The Prodigal Daughter.*

Wade, Tommy—see DUNDRUM.

1256. WAGRAM—One of Napoleon Bonaparte's favorite gray Arabian war stallions, named after the Battle of Wagram.

WAHAMA—see FLICKA.

Wakely, Jimmy—see SUNSET.

Walker, Clint—see BRANDY.

Wallace, Lew, author—see ALDEBARAN, ANTARES, ATAIR, EROS, MARS, RIGEL.

Wallen, Darrel—see MR. RYTHM.

"Wanted—Dead or Alive," television show—see RINGO.

1257. WAR ADMIRAL—The 1937 Triple Crown winner, sired by MAN O'WAR and owned by Samuel Riddle. The small seal-brown colt was also known as THE

MIGHTY ATOM and ADMIRAL. He was always difficult at the starting gate but liked to be the front runner. WAR ADMIRAL died in 1959.

1258. WAR PAINT—A well-known saddle bronc now mounted at the Hall of Fame at the Pendleton Round-Up grounds in Pendleton, Oregon. He was the first recipient of the Bucking Horse of the Year Award, and won it three times from 1956 to 1958.

1259. WAR PAINT—The pinto gelding mascot of the Kansas City Chiefs football team in the 1960s and 1970s.

Waring, Colonel George—see KLITSCHKA, MAX.

1260. WARREN—One of Union General Benjamin Butler's war chargers in the Civil War, a 16-hand spirited sorrel. Butler rode him in the review of the army in 1864 when Butler loaned his other horse, EBONY, to President Lincoln. The stallion EBONY bolted with the president when the artillery started up. Butler could not catch up with the president, but finally an orderly was able to catch and stop them.

1261. WARRIOR—The horse ridden in World War I by Lord Mottistone, who said WARRIOR was the luckiest horse in the war because he had played a decisive role in holding back the last offensive of the Germans.

1262. WARRIOR—Canadian General Jack Seely's bay warhorse in World War I. WARRIOR was a short-legged Thoroughbred foaled in 1908. He survived the war and lived to over 30 years of age.

1263. WASHINGTON—One of General Winfield Scott's war-horses, a bright sorrel.

Washington, George—see BLUESKIN, DOLLY (359), JACK (578), JACKSON, LEXINGTON (674), MAGNOLIA, NELSON, RANGER (951), ROYAL GIFT.

Washington, Martha—see FATIMA.

1264. WASHOE BAN—Writer Jack London's favorite riding horse. He rode this horse in 1906 to view San Francisco's fires after the big earthquake.

The Way of the Wild—see NORTHWIND.

Wayne, John—see BEAU, STEEL.

Webster, Daniel—see STEAMBOAT (1125).

Wellesley, Arthur—see COPENHAGEN.

Wellington, Duke of—see COPENHAGEN.

Wentworth, Lady—see SKOWRONEK.

Wescott, Edward Noyes, author—see DAVID HARUM'S BALKY HORSE.

West, James T.—see CACAO, DUKE (381).

West, Johnny—see THUNDERBOLT.

Westward the Women, movie—see STEEL.

1265. WHINNEY—The young filly that prehistoric Ayla befriends and tames in Jean Auel's books *Valley of the Horses, Mammoth Hunters,* and *Plains of Passage,* in her series *Earth's Children.* After killing the foal's mother in a trap, Ayla decides to tame the young animal in a time when most people still considered horses to be a source of food. Ayla rides WHINNEY without anything controlling her, but Jondalar has to ride WHINNEY's young son RACER with a halter and rope.

1266. WHIRLAWAY—The 1941 Triple Crown winner, a chestnut colt with three white socks and a white star, also known as WHIRLY, MR. LONGTAIL, and THE FLYING TAIL because of his unusually long tail. He was foaled in 1938 on Calumet Farm and had a bad disposition and was difficult to train. His jockey, Eddie Arcaro, who has ridden five Kentucky Derby winners, said that the horse was difficult to ride as he liked to veer to the outside, but that was fixed when the trainer cut off the horse's left blinker to help him focus on the inside. He liked to come from behind and run down the middle of the track. He was a spooky horse and had to be hand-walked around every racetrack he was to run on. WHIRLAWAY won the Kentucky Derby by 8 lengths, the Preakness by 5 ½ lengths, the Belmont by 3 lengths, and was the fifth horse to win the Triple Crown. He match-raced ALSAB, and while it looked like both crossed the line together, the win was given to ALSAB. He was to race at Pimlico in 1942, but everyone else dropped out, so he ran alone and won $10,000. He retired in 1943 at age 5 and died suddenly in 1953 from a rupture while in France.

1267. WHISKERY—The 1927 Kentucky Derby winner, a brown colt.

1268. WHITE BEAUTY—An albino Thoroughbred racehorse.

1269. WHITE CLOUD—The pony in Miram E. Mason's book *Lightning*.

1270. WHITE CLOUD—One of Eddie Dean's horses in early western movies.

1271. WHITE EAGLE—One of Buck Jones' movie horses.

WHITE FELLER—see SCOUT (1040).

1272. WHITE FLASH—Tex Ritter's white horse in early westerns. WHITE FLASH died in 1966 at age 25.

1273. WHITE FURY—Jack Hoxie's horse in silent western movies.

1274. WHITE STAR—The horse in Stan Steiner's book *The Little Horse.*

1275. WHITE SURREY—King Richard III's favorite mount, a white destrier, in William Shakespeare's play *King Richard III.* King Richard III is famous for saying, "A horse, a horse, my kingdom for a horse."

1276. WHITEY—One of Hoot Gibson's movie horses.

WHITEY—see OLD WHITEY.

Whitman, Dr. Marcus—see UNKNOWN HORSES (1236).

Wide Country, movie—see REX (976).

1277. WIDOW-MAKER—Pecos Bill's palomino stallion in cowboy tall tales. It is said that Bill fed his horse nitroglycerine and barbed wire and that the horse would buck anyone else who tried to ride him sky high.

"Wild Bill Hickok," television show—see BUCK-SHOT, JOKER.

Wild Is the Wind, movie—see FURY (466).

"Wild Wild West," television show—see CACAO, DUKE (381).

1278. THE WILDAIR MARE—Thought to be the dam of JUSTIN MORGAN, she was descended from a part-Thoroughbred part-Arabian stallion named WILDAIR.

Wilder, Laura Ingalls, author—see BARNUM, FLY, PATTY, PET (893), SKIP, TRIXY.

1279. WILDFIRE—The pony in the 1975 song "Wildfire," by Michael Murphy.

1280. WILDFIRE—The horse in George Eliot's book *Silas Marner* that Godfrey is forced to sell so that he can afford to marry. Before the sale to his brother is finalized, the brother takes the horse out hunting and the horse is killed in an accident.

1281. WILL SHRIVER—A well-known American Saddlebred horse.

Williams, Guy—see PHANTOM, TORNADO.

1282. WILLIE GROW—A light roan Philippine war pony that was ridden by Frederick Funston while in the Philippines in the early 1900s.

Wills, Chill—see FRANCIS.

1283. WILMA—A Belgian mare said to be as heavy as BROOKLYN SUPREME, 3,200 pounds.

Wilson, Whip—see SILVER BULLET.

WINCHESTER—see RIENZI.

Winchester, Major Charles Emerson III—see PEGASUS (887).

Winchester, '73, movie—see PIE (906).

The Wind in the Willows, book—see CYRIL.

1284. WING COMMANDER—A liver chestnut American Saddle Horse stallion that was the World Champion 5-gaited horse for 7 years in a row, from 1948 to 1954.

Winkfield, Jimmy—see ALAN-A-DALE.

Winkler, Hans—see HALLA.

1285. WINNIE—A strawberry roan mare ridden by highwayman Tom Faggus in R.D. Blackmore's book *Lorna*

Doone. WINNIE was loyal to Tom and would not let anyone else ride her.

Winnie-the-Pooh—see EEYORE.

1286. WINNING COLORS—The 1988 Kentucky Derby winner, a roan filly with a gray mane. She was the third filly to win the Kentucky Derby, after REGRET (1915) and GENUINE RISK (1980). Her jockey was Idahoan Gary Stevens.

1287. WINSTON—A police horse ridden by Queen Elizabeth II in ceremonial parades in the 1950s. They are portrayed together on the official seal for Lancashire, England.

1288. WINTERGREEN—The 1909 Kentucky Derby winner, a bay colt.

1289. WISP O'MIST—One of MISTY's foals in real life. MISTY is the Chincoteague pony from Marguerite Henry's book *Misty of Chincoteague.*

Wister, Owen, author—see MONTE (793).

1290. WITEZ II—A purebred Polish Arabian stallion saved by General George Patton and brought to the United States after World War II.

The Wizard of Oz, movie—see SYLVESTER.

The Wonder Book—see PEGASUS (886).

1291. WOODBURY MORGAN—One of JUSTIN MORGAN's three sons that helped to establish the Morgan Horse breed.

1292. WOODENHEAD—The horse in the animated movie *Journey Back to Oz.*

1293. WORTH—The 1912 Kentucky Derby winner, a brown colt.

1294. WORTHLESS—Dirty Sally Fergus's mule in the TV show "Dirty Sally."

1295. WOYCHECK—A successful dressage horse ridden by Harry Boldt.

Wrangler Jane—see PECOS.

1296. XANTHUS—One of the two immortal horses born of Zephyrus and the Harpy Podarge that drew Achilles' chariot in Greek mythology. The other horse was BALIUS. XANTHUS was said to have predicted his master's death after being scolded by him. The name means "dun" or "reddish yellow."

1297. XANTHUS—One of Hector's chariot horses. Their story is told in Homer's *Iliad*.

1298. XERXES—One of two horses belonging to the fat, jovial huntsman John Jorrocks in the popular fox-hunting novels written by Robert S. Surtees in the 1840s and 1850s. The other horse was AR-TERXERXES. ARTERXERXES was named that because when the horses were driven in tandem to the hunt, XERXES came first, and ARTERXERXES came "arter" XERXES.

Year of the Horse, book—see ASPERCEL.

1299. YOUNG BULROCK—The horse that is thought by a few to have been the sire of JUSTIN MORGAN. Most people agree that TRUE BRITON was the sire of JUSTIN MORGAN.

1300. ZACHREGARD—A 5-year-old Thoroughbred race mare that the Federal Bureau of Investigation purchased in 1989 to be an undercover agent at a New York racetrack. The FBI hoped that the undistinguished Thoroughbred would attract some illegal offers, but the horse ran too well. The FBI did, however, catch some criminals in the sting.

1301. ZANATON—Quarter Horse that was called the MEXICAN MAN O'WAR and was the sire of KING.

1302. ZAPE—An Arabian horse that was given to the president of Cuba by the king of Spain.

1303. ZARIF—One of several horses owned and trained by Karl Krall in Elberfeld, Germany, in the late 1800s and early 1900s that could do mathematics. Scientists could find no fraud in the demonstration. See also KLUGE HANS (644).

Zeitter, painter—see PIRATE.

Zephyrus—see BALIUS, XANTHUS (1296).

1304. ZEV—The 1923 Kentucky Derby winner, a brown colt. He did not run well in 1924 because a leg injury he had received was treated with the wrong kind of alcohol.

1305. ZINGARILLO—The 20-year-old racehorse ridden by Alicia Thornton in a match race in 1804. The other horse won. Mrs. Thornton always dressed very stylishly when racing her horses.

1306. ZIP POCKET—The Thoroughbred racehorse that set a world record for six furlongs in 1966.

Zola, Emile, author—see BATAILLE, NANA.

1307. ZOMBIE—Bing Crosby's first racehorse, which he got in 1935. Crosby is said to have been the first actor to own a racehorse.

"Zorro," television show—see PHANTOM (898), TORNADO.

SUBJECT INDEX

The index refers the reader to the entry number, not the page number, for the horse's name in the book. Most of the horses are listed only once in the index, so that, for example, a racehorse in a story will be listed only under LITERARY HORSES, not also under RACEHORSES, FLAT.

FOLKTALE HORSES (see also LITERARY HORSES)   117, 325, 414, 1024, 1046, 1277

HERO HORSES   870, 977, 1064, 1227

HORSE TAMERS' HORSES   306

KENTUCKY DERBY WINNERS   16, 17, 20, 39, 51, 57, 67, 71, 76, 103, 109, 110, 138, 166, 168, 189, 195, 197, 206, 228, 229, 238, 242, 250, 258, 265, 268, 297, 298, 319, 327, 331, 334, 339, 366, 367, 385, 399, 411, 425, 446, 448, 449, 475, 476, 482, 485, 487, 529, 550, 553, 556, 560, 573, 597, 602, 607, 611, 623, 638, 662, 668, 677, 697, 700, 704, 712, 722, 733, 759, 764, 794, 797, 813, 837, 851, 860, 861, 881, 890, 910, 912, 913, 924, 934, 969, 971, 986, 990, 1044, 1045, 1065, 1082, 1084, 1112, 1113, 1114, 1132, 1144, 1148, 1151, 1152, 1185, 1195, 1215, 1219, 1223, 1243, 1246, 1257, 1266, 1267, 1286, 1288, 1293, 1304

KNIGHTS' HORSES (see also WAR-HORSES, OTHER WARS)   63, 74, 512

LEGENDARY HORSES (see also MYTHOLOGICAL HORSES)   23, 29, 96, 150, 185, 188, 217, 376, 416, 512, 586, 649, 661, 866, 872, 942, 949, 1251

LITERARY HORSES (see also FOLKTALE HORSES, LEGENDARY HORSES, MYTHOLOGICAL HORSES)   13, 27, 45, 47, 61, 63, 66, 68, 77, 78, 84, 87, 93, 112, 119, 133, 135, 136, 145, 151, 154, 163, 176, 179, 182, 184, 187, 221, 224, 230, 231, 257, 259, 260, 266, 267, 270, 276, 292, 309, 311, 313, 324, 326, 329, 330, 336, 344, 355, 374, 377, 379, 389, 392, 395, 397, 400, 406, 409, 417, 434, 435, 440, 442, 444, 447, 463, 470, 471, 472, 474, 480, 486, 490, 494, 495, 503, 519, 523, 532, 562, 566, 572, 579, 595, 596, 612, 628, 632, 641, 650, 652, 659, 670, 678, 679, 681, 685, 687, 692, 693, 699, 715, 716, 723, 726, 739, 741, 761, 762, 772, 783, 784, 789, 793, 802, 804, 806, 814, 833, 838, 839, 842, 862, 863, 877, 878, 880, 891, 893, 897, 900, 902, 907, 908, 918, 943, 945, 949, 950, 967, 970, 985, 992, 995, 997, 1001, 1005, 1021, 1022, 1025, 1031, 1039, 1042, 1043, 1050, 1052, 1059, 1063, 1073, 1085, 1089, 1096, 1102, 1106, 1110, 1115,

1134, 1135, 1137, 1154, 1159, 1175, 1183, 1192, 1210, 1217, 1241, 1245, 1265, 1269, 1274, 1275, 1280, 1285, 1289, 1297, 1298

LONG HORSEBACK RIDES   481, 489, 729, 1028, 1048

MASCOT AND LOGO HORSES   171, 302, 825, 885, 888, 928, 1108, 1158, 1202, 1259

MILITARY PERSONALITIES' HORSES (see also WAR-HORSES)   33, 576, 592, 629, 1214, 1290

MOVIE HORSES   9, 10, 27, 46, 50, 58, 66, 68, 75, 83, 85, 86, 90, 91, 98, 102, 115, 122, 132, 137, 145, 147, 149, 153, 158, 160, 163, 169, 174, 181, 186, 193, 220, 223, 233, 239, 240, 245, 247, 251, 262, 286, 287, 290, 293, 300, 345, 357, 362, 364, 368, 372, 382, 415, 430, 438, 439, 444, 451, 455, 462, 466, 468, 488, 492, 499, 504, 506, 524, 533, 544, 559, 565, 583, 614, 627, 634, 635, 636, 645, 646, 652, 673, 679, 680, 684, 687, 688, 717, 738, 743, 766, 767, 769, 784, 785, 801, 803, 814, 815, 817, 845, 846, 869, 871, 874, 875, 906, 907, 915, 935, 939, 940, 946, 947, 948, 953, 958, 960, 965, 967, 970, 973, 976, 987, 989, 996, 998, 1003, 1011, 1016, 1017, 1019, 1030, 1041, 1067, 1070, 1071, 1074, 1075, 1076, 1077, 1095, 1096, 1099, 1116, 1121, 1122, 1123, 1127, 1133, 1143, 1147, 1149, 1153, 1156, 1157, 1160, 1168, 1170, 1180, 1184, 1193, 1194, 1196, 1197, 1201, 1206, 1270, 1271, 1272, 1273, 1276, 1292

MOVIE STARS', ACTORS', AND SPORTS STARS' HORSES   38, 54, 72, 100, 177, 278, 571, 651, 756, 882, 1143, 1173

MULES   194, 455, 870, 1018, 1211, 1294

MUSIC AND HORSES (SONGS, RECORD ALBUMS, AND SINGERS' HORSES)   443, 615, 654, 1143, 1279

MYTHOLOGICAL HORSES, CLASSICAL   2, 3, 12, 14, 15, 21, 40, 56, 81, 190, 244, 312, 335, 404, 407, 554, 658, 660, 735, 834, 886, 896, 904, 905, 938, 1131, 1296

605, 607, 611, 623, 625, 630, 638, 639, 662, 664, 668, 676, 677, 696, 697, 700, 702, 704, 712, 719, 722, 728, 730, 733, 759, 764, 770, 771, 775, 779, 794, 797, 808, 809, 811, 813, 823, 830, 835, 836, 837, 851, 859, 860, 861, 864, 876, 881, 890, 892, 895, 901, 910, 912, 913, 923, 924, 934, 954, 955, 969, 971, 982, 986, 990, 994, 1007, 1013, 1014, 1043, 1044, 1045, 1051, 1065, 1068, 1081, 1082, 1083, 1084, 1112, 1113, 1114, 1117, 1129, 1132, 1139, 1142, 1144, 1148, 1151, 1152, 1163, 1173, 1174, 1176, 1177, 1185, 1189, 1191, 1195, 1212, 1213, 1215, 1216, 1218, 1219, 1223, 1242, 1243, 1246, 1257, 1266, 1267, 1268, 1286, 1288, 1293, 1300, 1301, 1304, 1305, 1306, 1307

RACEHORSES, HARNESS 22, 43, 55, 108, 139, 180, 234, 318, 321, 341, 408, 443, 458, 501, 505, 507, 517, 587, 648, 654, 751, 821, 826, 916, 1080, 1093, 1120, 1190, 1198, 1224

RACEHORSES, STEEPLECHASE 4, 26, 59, 95, 130, 253, 277, 340, 383, 388, 410, 461, 516, 589, 656, 701, 731, 773, 788, 822, 827, 919, 968, 981, 1010, 1012, 1053, 1171, 1188, 1204, 1255

RADIO HORSES 41, 467, 873, 1037, 1180

RECORD-BREAKING HORSES (SIZE) 120, 191, 413, 431, 750, 796, 844, 1283

RELIGIOUS PERSONALITIES' HORSES 342, 526, 619, 621, 657, 787, 1226

RODEO HORSES 432, 765, 1049, 1124, 1187, 1258

ROYALTY'S HORSES 8, 28, 32, 42, 62, 69, 82, 104, 116, 207, 210, 243, 279, 285, 289, 295, 296, 340, 370, 371, 423, 469, 508, 509, 546, 548, 549, 569, 601, 655, 671, 694, 707, 709, 713, 730, 771, 776, 790, 852, 892, 929, 936, 1004, 1032, 1036, 1055, 1107, 1136, 1140, 1167, 1244, 1287

SETTLERS' AND FRONTIER HORSES (see also EXPLORERS' AND CONQUERORS' HORSES) 142, 183, 202, 580, 850, 854, 930, 1105, 1236

BOOKS FOR FURTHER READING

Adler, Larry. *Famous Horses in America.* D. McKay Co., 1979.

Alcock, Anne. *The Love of Horses.* Octopus Books, 1973.

Alcock, Anne. *The Love of Ponies.* Octopus Books, 1975.

Allusions: Cultural, Literary, Biblical and Historical—A Thematic Dictionary. Gale Research Co., 1982.

Amaral, Anthony. *The Fascinating Techniques of Training Movie Horses.* Wilshire, 1957.

Amaral, Anthony. *Movie Horses: Their Treatment and Training.* Bobbs-Merrill, 1967.

Anderson, C.W. *The Smashers.* Harper, 1954.

Bell, Robert E. *Dictionary of Classical Mythology.* ABC-CLIO, 1982.

Benford, Timothy B. *Royal Family Quiz and Fact Book.* Harper and Row, 1987.

Berman, Lucy. *Famous Horses.* Golden Press, 1972.

Blassingame, Wyatt. *His Kingdom for a Horse.* Books for Libraries Press, 1957.

Boyd, Mildred. *History in Harness: The Story of Horses.* Criterion Books, 1965.

Browder, Sue. *The Pet Name Book.* Workman Publishing, 1979.

Butterworth, W.E. *Soldiers on Horseback*. Norton, 1967.

Carlyon, Richard. *A Guide to the Gods*. Quill, 1981.

Carver, Sonora. *A Girl and Five Brave Horses*. Doubleday, 1961.

Champion, Bob, and Jonathan Powell. *Champion's Story: A Great Human Triumph*. Coward, McCann and Geoghegan, 1981.

Chew, Peter. *The Kentucky Derby: The First Hundred Years*. Houghton Mifflin, 1974.

The Complete Encyclopedia of Television Programs, 1947–1979. A.S. Barnes, 1979.

Crowell, Pers. *Cavalcade of American Horses*. Bonanza Books, 1951.

Denhardt, Robert Moorman. *The Quarter Running Horse: America's Oldest Breed*. University of Oklahoma Press, 1979.

Devereaux, Frederick L., Jr. *Famous American Horses: Twenty-one Steeplechasers, Trotters, Cow Ponies, Hunters, Flat Racers, Show Horses, and Battle Mounts That Made History*. Devon-Adair Co., 1975.

Downey, Bill. *Tom Bass, Black Horseman*. Saddle and Bridle, 1975.

Downey, Fairfax Davis. *Famous Horses of the Civil War*. Nelson, 1959.

Drager, Marvin. *The Most Glorious Crown*. Scribner's, 1975.

Duggan, Moira. *Horses*. Golden Press, 1972.

Dumas, Philippe. *The Lippizaners and the Spanish Riding School of Vienna*. Prentice-Hall, 1981.

Ellis, Peter Berresford. *A Dictionary of Irish Mythology*. ABC-CLIO, 1987.

Ensminger, M. Eugene. *The Complete Encyclopedia of Horses.* A.S. Barnes, 1977.

Evans, Edna Hoffman. *Famous Horses and Their People.* S. Greene Press, 1975.

Evans, Lawton B. *Famous Riders and Their Horses: Twelve Famous Rides in American History.* Milton Bradley Company, 1927.

Famous Saddle Horses: Stories About the Most Important Horses in the Early Days of the American Saddle Horse. Standard Printing Co., 1932.

Fetros, John G. *Dictionary of Factual and Fictional Riders and Their Horses.* Exposition Press, 1979.

Fetros, John G. *This Day in Sports.* Newton K. Gregg, 1974.

Galloping Off in All Directions: An Anthology for Horse Lovers. St. Martin's Press, 1978.

Geer, Andrew. *Reckless, Pride of the Marines.* Dutton, 1955.

Greenspan, Bud. *Play It Again, Bud!* P. H. Wyden, 1973.

Haley, Gail E. *Jack Jouett's Ride.* Viking, 1973.

Harrison, Jack. *Famous Saddle Horses and Distinguished Horsemen.* Harrison, 1933.

Heller, Julek, and Deirdre Headon. *Knights.* Schocken Books, 1982.

Henry, Marguerite. *Dear Marguerite Henry.* Rand McNally, 1969.

Henry, Marguerite. *A Pictorial Life Story of Misty.* Rand McNally, 1976.

Hodges, Margaret. *If You Had A Horse: Steeds of Myth and Legend.* Scribner's, 1984.

Humphreys, John O. *American Racetracks and Contemporary Racing Art.* South Bend Publishing Co., 1966.

Jobes, Gertrude. *Dictionary of Mythology, Folklore, and Symbols.* Scarecrow Press, 1961.

Jordan, Teresa. *Cowgirls: Women of the American West.* Anchor Press, 1982.

King, Roy, and Burke Davis. *World of Currier and Ives.* Bonanza Books, 1987.

Klimke, Reiner. *Ahlerich: The Making of a Dressage Horse.* Half Halt Press, 1986.

Lloyd, Ernest. *Animal Heroes.* Pacific Press, 1946.

Long, Matthew. *Wonderful World of Horses.* Octopus, 1976.

McIlvaine, Jane. *The Will to Win: The True Story of Tommy Smith and Jay Trump.* Doubleday, 1966.

Moody, Ralph. *Come On, Seabiscuit.* Houghton Mifflin, 1963.

Moody, Ralph. *Riders of the Pony Express.* Dell, 1958.

Nash, Jay Robert. *Motion Picture Guide.* Cinebooks, 1987.

New Larousse Encyclopedia of Mythology. Prometheus Press, 1972.

Porter, Willard P. *Thirteen Flat: Tales of Thirty Famous Rodeo Ropers and Their Great Horses.* Barnes, 1967.

Rawson, Christopher. *Inside the World of Horses.* Usborne, 1978.

Real Animal Heroes: True Stories of Courage, Devotion and Sacrifice. Sharp and Dunnigan Publications, 1988.

Reiss, David S. *M*A*S*H: The Exclusive Inside Story of TV's Most Popular Show.* Bobbs-Merrill, 1983.

Self, Margaret Cabell. *The Horseman's Encyclopedia.* A.S. Barnes, 1946.

Smith, Vian. *Grand National: a History of the World's Greatest Steeplechase Race.* A.S. Barnes, 1969.

Taggart, Jean E. *Pet Names.* Scarecrow Press, 1962.

Talmadge, Marian, and Iris Gilmore. *Six Great Horse Rides.* Putnam, 1967.

Taylor, Louis. *Harper's Encyclopedia for Horsemen: The Complete Book of the Horse.* Harper and Row, 1973.

Thayer, Bert Clark. *Whirlaway: The Life and Times of a Great Racer.* Duell, Sloan, and Pearce, 1946.

Tremain, Ruthven. *The Animal's Who's Who: 1,146 Celebrated Animals in History, Popular Culture, Literature and Lore.* Scribner's, 1982.

Vavra, Robert. *Vavra's Horses: Ten of the World's Most Beautiful Equines.* Morrow, 1989.

Watney, Marilyn, and Sanders Watney. *Horse Power.* Hamlyn, 1975.

Wear, Terri A. *Horse Stories: An Annotated Bibliography of Books for All Ages.* Scarecrow Press, 1987.

Wilding, Suzanne, and Anthony del Balso. *Triple Crown Winners: The Story of America's Nine Superstar Racehorses.* Parents Magazine, 1975.

Zimmerman, J.E. *Dictionary of Classical Mythology.* Harper and Row, 1964.

ABOUT THE AUTHOR

Terri A. Wear received her Master of Library Science degree from the University of Oregon. She has been a reference librarian in Idaho for over ten years. Her first book was *Horse Stories: An Annotated Bibliography of Books for All Ages* (Scarecrow, 1987).